SEDUCED BY THE WEST

SEDUCED
by the WEST

*Jefferson's America
and the Lure of the Land
Beyond the Mississippi*

LAURIE WINN CARLSON

IVAN R. DEE

Chicago 2003

SEDUCED BY THE WEST. Copyright © 2003 by Laurie Winn Carlson.
All rights reserved, including the right to reproduce this book or portions
thereof in any form. For information, address: Ivan R. Dee, Publisher, 1332
North Halsted Street, Chicago 60622. Manufactured in the United States
of America and printed on acid-free paper.

Library of Congress Cataloging-in-Publication Data:
Carlson, Laurie W., 1952–
    Seduced by the West : Jefferson's America and the lure of the land
beyond the Mississippi / Laurie Winn Carlson.
      p. cm.
    Includes bibliographical references (p.) and index.
    ISBN 1-56663-490-3 (acid-free paper)
    1. West (U.S.)—Discovery and exploration. 2. United States—
Territorial expansion. 3. Jefferson, Thomas, 1743–1826—Views on the
West (U.S.) 4. Lewis and Clark Expedition (1804–1806) 5. Explorers—
West (U.S.)—History—19th century. 6. Explorers—West (U.S.)—
Biography. 7. West (U.S.)—History—To 1848. I. Title.

F592 . C29 2003
978'.02—dc21   2002031259

To Terry

Contents

Preface

THE LEWIS AND CLARK EXPEDITION, otherwise known as
the Corps of Discovery or the Quest for the Western Sea, has become part of the founding myth of the American West, integral
to our explanations of how the nation extended to the Pacific
Ocean. It remains one of the most examined yet most mysterious
of the many events that shaped the West. Composed of two
young military men and a loyal band that included the best of
frontier backwoodsmen as well as a young mother, a baby, a black
slave, and a Newfoundland dog, the group's fortitude, ethics, and
courage were exceptional. Yet whenever the reasons for its epic
and harrowing journey must be explained, we find ourselves
awash in grey. We suppose the nation was pushing its natural
boundaries to both coasts—our Manifest Destiny, a journalist
later pointed out; or we imagine it was a challenge that simply
had to be met because it was there.

Why, indeed, were Lewis and Clark sent to the Pacific when
American ships out of Boston were already plying the waters off
the Pacific Northwest coast, trading, bargaining, bickering, and
even recording deeds to property they purchased there in the
land of mystery? For a nation less than thirty years old to wrest

the West from the established European powers who claimed territory there seemed an improbability. The Russians were well established along the north Pacific coast; so too, the British fur trade was moving down from the Canadian Rockies; and the Spanish had been up and down the Pacific coast for more than a century.

If we think of the Pacific Northwest and the Rocky Mountain interior as a land as remote as the moon, we envision Lewis and Clark as being somewhat akin to John Glenn, the first American astronaut to orbit the earth. And if we do that, it becomes clear that this was no effort to gather plants and rocks—it was meant to show other nations that Americans too could mount an expedition. Beyond that, it was a ploy to tempt the Spanish to react. By dangling the little band of highly visible, slow-moving explorers across the prairies, Spanish colonial forces might attack them, try to stop them, perhaps even kill them. Then everything would be in place for the greatest land grab in history. American forces were stationed along the southern borders of the United States, ready to move against Spanish holdings in Florida and what would become Texas.

Improbable that a president would use a brave and loyal man like Meriwether Lewis in such a way? Even John Glenn's fate might have become political fodder—John Kennedy and his administration planned to blame Cuba if any misfortune befell Glenn's mission, a fairly dangerous gamble. With the blame on Castro, Kennedy would have the excuse he needed to attack Cuba without the appearance of launching another Pearl Harbor. But, Glenn—like Meriwether Lewis—made it back safely, engaged in politics, and made his mark in government. Yet a few years after he returned, Lewis was dead. His former mentor, Thomas Jefferson, insisted it was an unfortunate suicide. In spite of his effort and sacrifice (at the time of his death, the government still owed him money for supplies he had purchased out of his own pocket for the expedition), Lewis is not buried at Arlington National Cemetery for military heroes. He was abandoned along a trail in Tennessee, his grave overgrown and forgotten until the present.

JEFFERSON, the Virginian under whose presidency the Louisiana Purchase extended the nation far into the West, actually knew very little about the region. He thought the Blue Ridge Mountains were the highest on the continent and that a huge mountain made of salt lay somewhere in the Great Plains. He believed that volcanoes were active in the upper Missouri, and he was nearly obsessed with obtaining bone remnants of a large mammoth he believed once existed in North America.[1]

Today Jefferson's Monticello home is regarded as the kickoff point for the Lewis and Clark trip west. That is where Jefferson studied, corresponded about, and planned Western exploration. Monticello housed his private collection of Indian memorabilia and artifacts as well as natural history specimens, replicating the practice of European aristocrats at the time who were enamored with science. Jefferson never traveled west, in fact seldom traveled at all except for semi-annual trips between his home and the nation's capital.[2]

Jefferson did, however, pay close attention to how he would be remembered in history. This interest led him to retain copies of letters (but only those that shaped the persona he wished to reveal) along with a variety of books and items that symbolized enlightened thinking. His foresight and effort has resulted in Jefferson becoming a touchstone for Western exploration. But the men who did the exploring, provisioning, organizing, and trekking were cut from far different cloth. None were wealthy, few left any papers for historians to pursue, and they had little ability to shape how history would remember them. Perhaps that is why so many have been forgotten. This book attempts to explore the wide range of players during this era of intrigue and possibilities.

The nation itself was only a few years old when the first attempts westward were initiated. The competitors—Russia, Spain, England, France—all would try to explore the West, and all for different reasons. Only one nation succeeded, but it was not always a simple task.

SEDUCED BY THE WEST

1

Away to the North Pacific

When I had dealings with the Cheyenne people, in the course of the summer of 1795 . . . I inquired of all if, in their long war marches toward the mountains, they had not discovered some river the waters of which might possibly flow to the setting sun. They told me that two years before, the Cheyenne and Kiowa . . . having crossed the mountains, they had come, after many days' journey, to the banks of a wide and deep river. . . . They discovered unknown savages . . . [who] answered that at the mouth of this river appeared a large body of water, the other bank of which was not visible; that the water rose and fell considerably at certain times of the day and night. . . .—Jean Baptiste Trudeau, voyageur[1]

MERIWETHER LEWIS and William Clark's epic journey from St. Louis to the Pacific shore has left an indelible mark on America's psyche. The two men enjoy a well-deserved, near mythical status. Yet they have been ignored as much as they have been exploited. I spent several years living in an area that takes its ties to the Lewis and Clark expedition seriously. In Lewiston, Idaho, along the Clearwater River, directly on their path to the Columbia River, it was impossible to ignore their passage through the region. The Nez Perce people, who contributed to the Corps's survival, have maintained a powerful cultural and political presence. Equal attention is paid to William Clark; the town of Clarkston, Washington, is linked by a bridge across the Snake River. As I shopped at Lewis and Clark Foods, bought a Chevrolet at Lewis and Clark Motors, and cooled off in the Sacajawea Lounge, it seemed as if the men and their camping trip were simply a Chamber of Commerce promotion. Falling under the sway of their journals, however, like nearly everyone who reads them, I became mesmerized by the simple language and fascinating events and began to pay attention to what they said. I was bitten by the bug of what Larry McMurtry rightly calls "our national epic."

After stopping at the re-created Fort Clatsop on the Oregon coast (it was a drizzling, typical Oregon-coast type of day—making it a lot like Lewis and Clark's descriptions), I began to wonder why no ship had come to pick up the exhausted expeditioners upon their arrival at the Pacific. Why, actually, had they come this far? Then, shocked as most people are to discover that Meriwether Lewis died under questionable circumstances, my curiosity intensified. I had to know the whole story. How did that cagey genius, Thomas Jefferson, orchestrate events from rural Virginia? What did the fiery-tempered Spaniards, laden with honor and bureaucracy, think of it all? And, amid a swirl of frontier intrigue, why did Lewis and Clark return to find that the former vice president, the army's commanding general, and perhaps even the president himself were under scrutiny for attempting to divide the nation, West from East? That they might have returned from the Pacific coast to a nation divided and under different allegiances is stunning. For all of us who take the Lewis and Clark epic seriously, the tapestry of events and people reveals the complexity of history at the dawn of the nineteenth century, as the western half of the continent drew interest like a magnet.

ANYONE who has spent the day on a cross-continent airline flight laments the time it takes to cross the vast expanse that stretches from the Atlantic to the Pacific. From the Mississippi to the Pacific, the terrain changes considerably by the hour, as does the weather. On arrival, as one stretches and groans, complaining of the hardship of being stuck in an uncomfortable seat, and impatient over all the time "wasted" in flight, it is hard not to hold in awe those who paddled up rivers and hiked over this very same land. And while Lewis and Clark's expedition might first come to mind, there were many other attempts to cross North America. The people came from a variety of nations and took their chances for a variety of reasons; some were forgotten, others failed. There may have been several attempts that remain undiscovered, as failed efforts were quietly concealed or ignored. Upon seeing how many people had gone before them, it becomes clear that Lewis and Clark were able to accomplish the feat because they followed where others had already blazed a trail.

One might say the first attempt came more than two centuries earlier. In 1576 John Oxenham, a colleague of the famous English pirate Francis Drake, sailed to Panama, unloaded guns and munitions, and trekked overland to the Pacific Ocean. On shore his crew set to, built a serviceable watergoing craft, and captured a Spanish coastal ship loaded with 38,000 pesos. At the same time Drake was also at sea, wending his way up the Pacific coast a year later, going as far as northern California. While Oxenham did not cross the continent, exactly, he did reach the Pacific.[2]

The Pacific Ocean was under the domain of the Spanish crown, and though ships had spent centuries crossing and recrossing what the Spanish called the South Sea, the western coast of North America was not well known even by the late eighteenth century. Spanish ships ventured north along the Baja California coast and farther, but the strong currents headed southward. Exploration in the age of sailing ships was limited by the direction of winds and currents. It was difficult to make headway going north along lower California's rugged coast, and there was little to sustain crews if they stopped on land. More important, there was no gold or silver, and the small Indian settlements did not make for a strong source of labor. Spanish explorers were interested in minerals and people to mine them, and the California coast offered neither.

The Mississippi River had already been well explored, named, and claimed, and became central to whoever would control North America. Spain and France had played cat and mouse on the Mississippi for generations, beginning with Robert Cavalier, Sieur de La Salle, a French adventurer who trekked down the Mississippi Valley for France in the 1680s. He reached the Gulf of Mexico and named the entire region Louisiana, after Louis XIV, King of France.

La Salle had long sought a route across the North American continent to Asia but was distracted by an ambitious plan to conquer Spanish holdings in Mexico. He proposed a plan to Louis XIV that incorporated two hundred Frenchmen, fifteen thousand Indians, and as many privateers as could be recruited. The king liked the idea and provided men, ships, and cash. But La Salle was not an easy man to get along with, and his men frequently balked. Disasters abounded as well: ships went aground or were lost at sea, crews perished from sickness and drowning, and pirates captured a ship and supplies.

When the Spanish at Madrid heard of La Salle's travels, they sent eleven expeditions to find him; none succeeded. Failing to locate the mouth of the Mississippi by sea, La Salle had mistakenly put ashore in what is now Texas and attempted to set out overland. Eventually he was killed by two of his men while trekking from Matagorda Bay to the mouth of the Mississippi.[3]

FRANCE'S North American holdings had drained the royal treasury as a result of the Seven Years' War (called the French and Indian War in the colonies). To ease its burden, France ceded its Louisiana holdings west of the Mississippi River to Spain in a secret treaty signed on November 3, 1762. Louisiana was a financial liability for either European power, yet both maintained a hold on it only to prevent the English from gaining control of the Mississippi River. As a source of colonial wealth, Louisiana was worthless; as a vacant buffer zone to protect incursions into Mexican mines, it was invaluable.[4] In the eighteenth century the future political, economic, and social worlds of North America were changed completely with a quill pen in the staterooms of Europe, as colonial holdings were transferred between various monarchs. Border animosities that had gone on for decades between French and Spanish factions suddenly were nullified, allegiances expected to change, and all without a fight—or even a comment—from those living and governing in America.

The Spanish government's policy controlled trade and manufacturing in all of the crown's colonial holdings, including America. Strict regulations against importing non-Spanish goods or manufactured items for use in the colonies, or exporting products by Spanish colonists to other countries, was forbidden. Since Spanish goods had to travel along strictly approved and defined trade routes, transport took longer and cost more. As a result Spanish colonists began to rely on contraband, which accelerated smuggling and the consequences that accompanied it.

French traders continued to make incursions into Spanish lands, trading guns and goods with Indians. When Indian tribes like the Comanches, newcomers to the Southwest and enemies of Spain's other Indian allies, adopted French guns and captured Spanish horses, violence escalated. Spain's goal in the New World was not to annihilate the Indians but to turn them into taxpaying Christians. The best way to avert bloodshed was to keep out foreign elements. To keep French traders (and their traded guns) out, in the 1750s Madrid declared that any foreigner venturing to trade in New Mexico would receive the death penalty. This reduced trade to a single lifeline, the royal road from Chihuahua to the northern settlements in America.[5]

Meanwhile Spanish ships were edging north along the Pacific coast. In 1774 Juan Pérez took command of the *Santiago* out of San Blas, now in Mexico. His purpose was to establish Spanish claims to the north Pacific region by going ashore, erecting a cross, and burying a bottle containing a written claim to the area. He was also to ascertain whether Russian fur traders had encroached on the region, as rumored. He stopped at what is today Vancouver Island, anchoring off Nootka. Rough weather prevented the crew from going ashore to erect a formal claim, but Indians paddled out to the ship and began trading, obtaining several silver spoons from the crew. Later, when British claims to the area conflicted with Spain's, those spoons proved Spain's prior claim to the coast. Pérez was followed the next year by Bruno de Hezeta and Juan Francisco de la Bodega y Quadra, in two ships.

Hezeta and twenty armed soldiers made it ashore at what is now Port Greenville on the Washington coast, where they erected a cross of possession for Spain. Farther north in the other ship, Bodega y Quadra sent six men ashore to collect casks of fresh drinking water. About three hundred Indians emerged from the underbrush and, in a surprise attack, murdered the party of Spaniards while the men aboard ship watched.[6] Several Indians then paddled out in canoes and attempted to board the ship by climbing the sides. The Spaniards resorted to muskets and a swivel gun to stave off the attack, killing several Indians. The Spanish presence in the Pacific Northwest had begun, a presence that was never entirely successful nor peaceful.

The region was minimally important to Spain's far-flung empire until English crews sailing with Capt. James Cook discovered the valuable sea otter fur trade from the north Pacific coast to China, then controlled by the Russians. Spain bristled over news of Cook's third voyage, which threatened to open trade with the Spanish settlements along the coast of western Mexico and California. Spanish officials wrangled among themselves over whether to send out a force to arrest and prosecute Cook, who had sailed from London in 1776. Interference might be problematic because Britain's American colonies were in revolt; nevertheless King Carlos III ordered ships built in Peru to find Cook in the Pacific. But the force did not set out until three years after Cook left Boston, just as Cook's ships (now minus the unfortunate Cook, who was murdered at Kealakekua Bay) left Hawaii for Nootka and a cargo of sea otter furs they would take to China. Cook's men had no idea that Spanish warships were after them. The Spanish ships were outfitted with 14 cannons, 15 swivel guns, and an ample supply of cannonballs, powder, muskets, and swords. Of the 205 crewmen, 39 were marine artillerymen. Spain was serious but too slow to catch the English.[7] If they had intercepted Cook's crew at that point, the fur trade between the Bering Strait and Canton could have gone unnoticed for much longer.

But such was not the case. After the English crew returned, the news circulated about the explosive potential for profits, and ships from England and America began sailing to Nootka for furs. Russians too had been quick to settle in Alaska, and the small, isolated region was soon torn by geopolitical European rivalries. Spain hurried to establish a pseudo-colony at Nootka, replete with missionaries, settlers, and cattle as well as military personnel to secure its claims to the region.[8] And in early 1792 Spanish settlers established Núñez Gaona at Neah Bay, in present-day Washington State, with about ten houses and several gardens as well as a bakery, kiln, and blacksmith shop. Cows, sheep, goats, and pigs rounded out this first European settlement west of the Rocky Mountains on land that would eventually become part of the United States. For a time, however, the Spanish settlements in the Pacific Northwest were heavily armed and reinforced with thick log palisades and walls, replete with cannons that were fired nightly to discourage Indian attacks.

James Cook's scientific forays—he circumnavigated the globe three times—lent such esteem to British science that other countries quickly mounted competing efforts, combining science, espionage, and commercial interests. In 1786 France sent out a circumnavigation expedition emulating Cook, under the command of Jean-François de Galoup, Comte de la Pérouse. La Pérouse and his corps of scientists stopped on the Alaskan coast before continuing down the California coast. From La Pérouse, Spanish officials learned that Russian fur traders were encroaching eastward across the Bering Sea. La Pérouse continued his trek, calling at Botany Bay in Australia before he was forever lost at sea.⁹ Although no French attempts were made to establish a port for fur trading in the north Pacific, La Pérouse's voyage stirred fears in Spain that other nations might encroach on their interests there.

Spain's policy of keeping its colonial settlements and excursions secret came back to haunt its plans to retain control of the Pacific coast. Because nothing had been allowed to appear in print about Spanish voyages and discoveries there, other countries did not believe Spanish claims. A cross and a bottle may have sufficed for unwanted areas, but as the popularity of sea trade exploded and as England's navy grew in strength, other nations began challenging Spain's claims on the Pacific coast. Ships' logs and records were indeed state secrets—Spain kept them hidden in archives in Madrid, unavailable even to other Spanish explorers. Thus Spanish explorers had no idea who had gone before them, and other countries had no clear references or information about the primacy of Spanish claims. When Cook's expeditions returned, their logs were carefully scrutinized for anything the English navy wanted to keep secret, then published and widely disseminated. Everyone knew what the Englishman and his floating laboratory had discovered, and such knowledge provided a basis for future claims against aggressions by other trading entities. Spain's reluctance to disseminate information to other nations only weakened its credibility.

The need to publish reports about government expeditions, along with a growing interest in science and natural history, resulted in a Spanish attempt to compete with Cook's scientific explorations. In 1789 the Spanish Naval Scientific Exploring Expedition, headed by Alejandro Malaspina, left Cádiz for the Pacific. Well outfitted, the 2 ships and 102 crewmen even brought a harpsichord on board. By 1791 they were in the Pacific, departing from Acapulco for the northwest coast. A five-year venture supported by Carlos III, Malaspina's expedition collected natural history specimens, conducted experiments, and developed maps and sketches of places and people the entourage encountered. Malaspina's legacy fell into obscurity, however, because upon his return to Madrid he challenged the government's New World policies, which he thought stifled economic development of the Spanish settlements there. He advised that Spain open trade rather than adhere to mercantilism. His comments, as well as his involvement in palace intrigue between Queen María Luisa and Prime Minister Manuel de Godoy, won him a charge of treason. He was imprisoned for eight years before Napoleon prevailed, winning exile for Malaspina to Parma, where he died in 1810. His records and trip journals were confiscated and publication plans abandoned. Some records remained lost until the late twentieth century.[10]

American entrepreneurs were less interested in scientific exploration in the Pacific than they were in the potential profits from trade. John Ledyard, a crew member with Cook, published his own account of the trade. Although he could not obtain financial backing for a ship of his own, others quickly jumped onto the proposal. In 1786 the *Grand Turk* of Salem, Massachusetts, returned to New England touting a highly profitable venture in the Pacific fur trade. The arrival of these first ships laden with huge profits from the northern Pacific was momentous. The New England coast had slid into financial doldrums after the Revolution, and the news that profits were possible—even if at a great distance—invigorated the region. Merchants quickly created a triangular trade: manufactured goods were shipped from New England to the Pacific coast, exchanged for sea otter furs which were then taken to Canton, whereupon Chinese goods were brought back to New England.

THE AMERICANS, newly freed from the English, were quick to send west one of their own—quietly. In December 1789 the War Department sent Lt. John Armstrong from his post on the Ohio River to ascend the Missouri River in an attempt to reach the Pacific Ocean.[11] Armstrong had grown up in Pennsylvania and had served in the Continental Army under Washington. He had first-hand experience working with the Marquis de Lafayette and the explorer George Rogers Clark as well as General Anthony Wayne, and also knew James Wilkinson, who served under Wayne. When the army disbanded in 1784 after the Revolutionary War, he joined the first U.S. Regiment and was sent to secretly explore Western lands. He got no farther than St. Louis, but in doing so he laid a path for Lewis and Clark, who would follow with another military effort fifteen years later. Armstrong was not popular on the frontier because, like Alexander Hamilton and the Federalists, he sought to eliminate squatters from frontier lands.

Spain also tried unsuccessfully to find an overland route, years before Lewis and Clark. When France gave Louisiana to Spain in order to prevent the English from taking the rest of the continent at the close of the Seven Years' War, Spain realized the value of an overland route through their northern holdings. A route to Alta California that would seal off incursions into California and Mexico would be invaluable, and northern Louisiana offered the potential for the creation of that route. Spain aimed to keep foreigners out of Spanish colonial holdings in order to protect its mercantilist economic program. For decades Spain had attempted to stave off energetic efforts by foreign interests to supply Spain's colonies with cheaper foreign goods. But even for Spanish bureaucrats, smuggling offered a profitable sideline. Thus the greatest threat from encroaching Canadian traders from the north were the pots, pans, and liquor they toted, and the loyalties such trade goods fostered among the powerful Indian nations Spain needed as allies.

In the early 1790s the Spanish governor of Louisiana, Baron de Carondelet, in New Orleans, and his lieutenant governor, Zenon Trudeau, in St. Louis, tried to push Spanish exploration into the upper Missouri region in response to British encroachments near the Mandan Indian villages, about eighteen hundred miles north of St. Louis. Carondelet offered a $3,000 prize to the first person to reach the Pacific coast and return under the Spanish flag. In response, the Missouri Company, a private exploration and trade company, organized with the support of Carondelet and Trudeau. It was a group of merchants who agreed to build a series of trade posts between St. Louis and the Pacific in exchange for exclusive trading rights from Spain. The company made several attempts to send men and merchandise up the Missouri River to the Mandans, but the attempts were expensive failures.

In 1795 the company sent thirty men and four pirogues, at a cost of $100,000, upriver under James Mackay, a Scot who left the British fur trade and came south for better opportunities. Mackay brought John Evans as his lieutenant. Evans, a Welshman, was a British "explorer," said to have come to Louisiana in search of an elusive band of Indians believed to be descended from Welsh explorers thought to have been in North America in 1170. While a one-man quest for Welsh Indians appeared innocuous, even foolish, the Spanish took no chances on an oddly placed individual who just might be a British agent. Lieutenant

Governor Trudeau, in charge of St. Louis, claimed that Evans breached Spanish etiquette; he jailed him for two years. Eventually Trudeau changed his mind, realizing that Spain might benefit from Evans's search for the Welsh Indians as long as he did so under the Spanish flag. When Mackay set out on his northward expedition for the Missouri Company, Evans went along as his right-hand man.

Mackay's party took four pirogues of trade goods—one for the Sioux, one for the Arikaras, a third for the Mandans, and the fourth filled with goods for the Rocky Mountain tribes they expected to meet on their way to the Pacific. The entourage was also well armed with $15,000 worth of weapons. Rowing against the current while guarding the merchandise from every tribe they met proved taxing. The Otos and Omahas made progress difficult, particularly the Omaha chief Black Bird, who tried to keep the men and goods from going to tribes farther upriver. The party was delayed long enough for winter to set in and the river to freeze, halting their progress until spring.

Meanwhile Indians informed Mackay that British fur men had built a post among the Mandans; no time could be lost. To dislodge the British trappers among the Mandans, Mackay sent Evans ahead overland with a party of men and goods. Evans was given written instructions as to how he should conduct himself and his expedition. He was to continue beyond the Mandans to the Pacific in Mackay's stead. His instructions closely resembled those Thomas Jefferson would give to Meriwether Lewis seven years later.

The document, dated January 28, 1796, was essentially "explorer boilerplate," similar to Empress Catherine's instructions to Capt. Joseph Billings as he set out across Siberia, instructions which were based on Peter the Great's instructions to Vitus

Bering in 1728 and 1741.[12] During this period of rivalry and expansion on the seas, "exploring" usually meant finding an unseen route to another country's holdings, reconnoitering their strength and position while wooing the local peoples with trade goods, thereby paving the way for a later attempt to take over the area's trade and territory.

To provide accountability to those who funded and sent out such explorer-spies, diaries and journal logs were an imperative part of the expedition. Writing detailed logs made these fearless, hardy men (who almost never spoke of their ultimate political purpose) feel as if they indeed were on a scientific mission, while providing data that could later be scrutinized for key information. Evans was ordered to keep a daily journal in which he was to record "the route, distance, latitude and longitude . . . also the winds and weather." Such information would be vital for naval interests. It would never be shared with other explorers, in the secretive Spanish style. Evans was also to keep a second journal of notes about "all minerals, vegetables, timber, rocks, flintstone, territory, production, animals, game, reptiles, lakes, rivers, mountains, portages, with their extent and location; and the different fish and shellfish which the waters may contain." He was to record data about Indian groups—their numbers, manners, customs, government, language, and religion.[13]

Further, Evans was charged with charting a map of the Missouri River, even though he was to go by land. He was instructed to travel discreetly, to remain vigilant for Indian attacks yet never appear aggressive to those he encountered. He was urged to catch a live specimen of any unknown animal he encountered, which was to be shipped back for examination. If such a thing existed in the Rockies, Evans was to bring back a unicorn.

Once he reached the Pacific, Evans was to inquire from Indians as to the location of Russian settlements and determine how far inland they had come and how prevalent they were along the coast. He was urged not to spark conflict with the Russians, which might endanger him, and was to return overland, by a different route if possible, in order to gain further knowledge of the region.

Evans was to make sure to tell all Indians he met that Spain, "who is the protector of all the white and red men," had heard of them "and their needs, and desiring to make them happy" would soon be sending necessities to them. The trip was extremely important, Evans was reminded, not only to Spain but "to the universe," and would be a bold effort. To protect his claim to discovery, he should return with some physical evidence taken from the Pacific, such as salt water shells or sea otter skins.[14]

Evans was never instructed to return by sea. On the contrary, Mackay told him he would probably encounter ships from the United States and might propose to assist them by offering to bring back letters from the crews, which the Missouri Company would forward from St. Louis.[15] Evans was to tell no one of his trip, keeping his discoveries and notes secret. Upon his return to St. Louis, he was to give his notes only to the head of the company or to the Spanish governor.

In February 1796 Evans and two men set out from Mackay's stranded encampment over frozen ground, but after three hundred miles a Sioux war party forced them to return to Fort Charles. Evans set out again in June, as before, but this time drawing a careful map as he went. (Later, Jefferson sent the same map to Meriwether Lewis as he set out on Evans's trail.) He arrived to a warm reception at the Mandan villages where he routed the North West Company Canadians who were trading there, lowering the British flag and rechristening the post Fort

Mackay. During Evans's six-month stay, more British traders arrived, this time from the North West Company's rival, the Hudson's Bay Company. The Indian trade turf was contested not only between nations but between aggressive fur company competitors as well. When Evans's presence continued to disrupt British trade, however, the Indians resisted. He raised the Spanish flag to establish his authority, but he had run out of trade goods. After a cold winter, his health too was failing. He returned to St. Louis after being gone for two years.

Meanwhile the Missouri Company was in financial straits: the Spanish government had not provided their promised funding. Evans reported that he now believed there were no Welsh Indians up the Missouri, as the languages spoken by the peoples he met contained no Welsh words. He moved to New Orleans where he took up residence with the new Spanish governor Manuel Gayoso de Lemos, hoping to launch a career as a Spanish agent. Shortly after, Evans died at the age of twenty-eight, reportedly from alcoholism.[16] Someone else would have to complete the overland trek to the Pacific.

John Evans came closest to accomplishing what Meriwether Lewis was to begin four years later. And while Mackay and Evans's efforts did not successfully bring them to the Pacific, Spain would do their best to make sure that no other country followed suit.

DURING Thomas Jefferson's first summer as secretary of state in George Washington's cabinet, problems for the United States emerged from an unlikely sector of the globe. Far off in the northern Pacific, on Vancouver Island, a controversy smoldered over control of the Nootka Sound. Spain and Britain were fighting over fur posts in the north Pacific, and Britain went so far as

to ask Washington for permission to move British troops overland across America to fight the Spanish in the Pacific Northwest. Washington refused without hesitation, thinking that one
day he might have to rout the British soldiers from U.S. turf.[17]

Spain's economic power in Europe was declining by the late
eighteenth century, a consequence of continued warfare and
shrinking revenues from the colonies, making it difficult to expand or protect North American claims. Juan Pérez had been to
Nootka in 1774, claiming it for Spain, but Cook had anchored
there in 1778, affording the British an opening to push their
claim as well. After Cook's expedition, rumors reached Spain that
American and British ships planned to enter the Pacific fur trade,
spurred on by news of the untapped market in sea otter furs. Russian outposts were growing too: by 1784 a permanent settlement
had been established on Kodiak Island, and rumors spread that
five hundred Russians had settled in the region. Spain attempted
to protect its claims to Nootka and the entire area, sending expeditions by sea to quickly establish a settlement. In 1789 Estéban
José Martinez landed at Nootka with two ships. He quickly built
a settlement called Fort San Miguel, which consisted of about ten
buildings, including the commandant's house—a two-story Spanish colonial dwelling, replete with second-story porch and white-
washed exterior. To help with the building of the Nootka
settlement, twenty-nine Chinese laborers taken from an English
ship captured in the Pacific were put to work. The settlement
grew by fits and starts, however, and was never entirely safe from
the Indians, who continued depredations whenever the opportunity arose.

In 1790 Martinez quarreled with two British seafarers who
arrived to trade at Nootka. He seized their ships, and when the
news reached London it inflamed public sentiment against Spain.

The incident offered an opportunity to jump into a fight; Parliament immediately voted for funds for war.

For the United States, operating under a freshly crafted constitution, Nootka was trouble. Although Nootka itself was of little value, the claim to control of the coast from California to Alaska was important. Nevertheless, when Britain suggested that they would wish to move troops across America to fight in Spanish Louisiana if war developed, President Washington responded with his doctrine of neutrality—the United States would stay out of other nation's conflicts. Affairs in Europe were far more significant to Spain and Britain anyway—the Bastille had just been stormed in Paris, and there were fears that such mass anarchy might spread. With no allies interested in fighting over Nootka, Spain agreed to share the Pacific Northwest with the British and thus avoid war. The 1790 agreement, known as the Nootka Convention, was a landmark in Pacific history; it marked Spain's relinquishment of sovereignty on the Pacific coast.[18] It was not a well-defined document, however, so negotiators from both countries met on site at Nootka to work out the details of the convention. Nothing resulted from the meeting except a return to Europe, where Spain and England had been thrown into an unlikely alliance over fears of a spreading French Revolution. But England got what it wanted in the Pacific Northwest: access. And with Spain preoccupied in Europe and unable to maintain its settlement at Nootka, England did not need to establish settlements there.

In 1790 an American ship out of Boston, the *Columbia Rediviva*, under Capt. Robert Gray, arrived home from the Pacific coast. Gray was greeted with a hero's welcome; the *Columbia* was the first American ship to circumnavigate the globe. While the damaged cargo of Chinese tea did little to repay the owners' original investment of $49,000, the voyage was a significant achievement and certainly not ignored along the shipping coast of the new nation. Gray stayed in Boston only seven weeks before embarking on another trip to the Pacific Northwest. This time he discovered the mouth of a huge river which sailors had long known existed but were never able to find. He named it the Columbia River, after his ship, and claimed it for the United States. After trading along the coast, he forged a friendship with the Spaniard Juan Francisco de la Bodega y Quadra, who was posted at Nootka, where the *Columbia* was being repaired. Bodega y Quadra treated Gray and his crew to a dinner described later by one of Gray's crewmen: "Fifty four persons sat down . . . and the plates, which was *solid silver* was shifted five times, which made 270 plates!" The Americans were delighted with such formal hospitality from the Spanish, so much so that in 1794 Gray named his Massachusetts-born son Robert Don Quadra Gray.[19]

IN 1793 the American John Kendrick purchased land from the Spanish at Nootka. The legal land deeds remained in the government's files—in fact they probably crossed Thomas Jefferson's desk, arriving in the State Department while he was secretary of state in Washington's cabinet. Jefferson might have been surprised that Americans were locating in the north Pacific, but he knew of the local goings-on. Ships from Boston, Connecticut, and Philadelphia continued to ply the Pacific trade routes with little interference. In 1791 thirty-two ships from the United States, Spain, and Britain were trading on the Northwest coast.[20]

The most valuable asset the Pacific Northwest might have possessed—a passage to the Atlantic—had not been found; in fact, its existence was now clearly refuted. American attention was turning to the Floridas. Americans had been illegally settling and trading in Spanish-held East Florida when a new governor, Vincente Manuel de Zespedes, toured the region in 1787 and wrote that the American backwoods folk were "nomadic like Arabs . . . and distinguished from savages only by their color, language, and the superiority of their depraved cunning and untrustworthiness."[21] The Treaties of Paris in 1783 had put Spain in control of the Floridas again, taking them from Britain at the end of the American Revolution. To keep Americans out of Spanish land, in 1784 Spain closed the lower Mississippi River to all but Spanish trade. Residents of Kentucky and Tennessee were infuriated, having nowhere else to ship their produce. They relied on shipping their flour, bacon, and other products down to the Gulf on flatboats. If they had no way to get their agricultural products to market, there was little incentive to plant or even to remain U.S. citizens. Excited talk swirled about the frontiers, where some Americans were eager to go to war with Spain while others were just as eager to secede from the United States and become Spanish subjects for commercial purposes.

After assessing the situation, Spain decided to abandon its policy of keeping Louisiana as a vacant buffer zone between Mexican mines and the aggressive Americans. It was impossible to keep the hungry, hardy Yankee squatters out of Louisiana, so Spain began encouraging immigration to Louisiana to those who were willing to become Spanish subjects. In return, immigrants received free trade access to river shipping and land. A scattering of Americans immigrated into Louisiana under these conditions. Daniel Boone is a well-known example of one frontiersman who became a naturalized Spaniard in order to settle on land there. Knowing that Americans would never be loyal to Spain no matter how lucrative the offer, Jefferson wrote to President Washington that the liberal immigration policy would not hurt the United

States. Shrewdly he noted that Spain's policy could be "the means of delivering to us peaceably, what may otherwise cost us a war."[22]

Population was increasing in the Western regions as a virtual baby boom ensued after the Revolution. Kentucky, which became a state in 1792, soared from 12,000 inhabitants in 1783 to 221,000 by 1800. Yet all of Spanish Louisiana had a population of only 50,000 by 1800.[23] One Spanish official commented that the Americans would take Louisiana in their bedrooms, not on the battlefield. It clearly looked as if that would be the case.

Yet even immigrants still could not travel to the Mexican interior to trade—the Spanish death penalty stood. Many challenged the law, and it was difficult to intercept everyone in the vast expanse of the Southwest. Those with financial backing could try to smuggle goods, but for those who had little to lose but their life, catching wild horses was a profitable venture. Several Americans bribed or risked their way past the Spanish patrols and went into Texas and Oklahoma to catch wild horses, which were herded back east and driven downriver. Flatboat men brought cargo downstream from Kentucky and then sold the cargo as well as the boat, which was taken apart for the lumber. The stranded boatmen would buy wild Spanish horses and ride them back home north, using this best mode of transport until the invention of the steam engine.

The Nootka Convention had ended the dispute over the northern Pacific and relinquished Spain's claim to sovereignty there. Spain eventually abandoned her holdings on the Northwest coast while England increased trade there but did not establish ownership of the region. Sovereignty in the area had changed, no longer relying on bottled documents but rather on occupancy. Without settled colonists, any given area was up for grabs. Even though the Pacific Northwest was distant from European settlements, the change in how ownership was held and maintained in the face of international challenges there established a precedent. As the historian David Lavender explains, "Far-off Nootka planted one of the seeds, though only one, that shortly would blossom into the Louisiana Purchase."[24]

Spain had known it was inescapable. Five years before the Nootka Convention ended Spain's autonomy in the northern Pacific, Viceroy Flórez of New Spain had written to Madrid in 1788, "We should not be surprised if the English colonies of America, republican and independent, put into practice the design of discovering a safe port on the South Sea [Pacific Ocean] and try to sustain it by crossing the immense land of this continent above our possessions of Texas, New Mexico and the Californias. . . . Obviously this is a feat that would take many years, but I truly believe that as of now we ought to try to elude its effects."[25]

Clearly Spain recognized that an expedition such as that of Lewis and Clark's was inevitable.

2

To the West by East: John Ledyard's Venture

What fate intends is always a secret; fortitude is the word.
—John Ledyard, Paris, 1786[1]

ANY STORY about exploration in the Pacific Northwest must include the most exciting, eccentric—and ignored—figure of John Ledyard. It was Ledyard, a wildly adventurous Connecticut native, who discovered the profitable yet secret fur trade the Russians had established with China in the late eighteenth century. It was Ledyard who opened the American sea trade to the northern Pacific coast, which led to the discovery of the Columbia River by the American Robert Gray. And it was John Ledyard, unsung hero, who laid the groundwork for the Lewis and Clark expedition.

The eldest of four children, Ledyard's father was a dashing sea captain involved in the West India trade. He died at sea at the age of thirty-five, and young John found himself living with his grandfather, who promptly sent him to school with the hope that he would someday practice law. The founder of Dartmouth College admitted John as a favor to the grandfather, and the young man arrived on campus dressed in "large, loose, Turkish breeches," riding in an unusual carriage, loaded with fabrics he planned to use in crafting stage costumes.[2]

Drama was Ledyard's love, but he decided instead to become a missionary to the Indians, one of the more dangerous and exciting occupations of the day. He enrolled at Dartmouth for less than a full year, spending three and a half months of that time investigating the Indian tribes living along the Canadian border. Upon his return to campus, he decided to quit school completely. With the help of a few friends, he embarked on a suitably attention-getting way to exit college: by felling a fifty-foot tree, hewing it into a canoe, and launching the craft into the Connecticut River. He floated 140 miles downstream, surprising and puzzling bystanders until he arrived at his uncle's home. Clad in bear skin, Ledyard shocked his relatives who believed him to be at college, studying seriously to make something of himself.[3]

His college career forgotten, his relatives refused to fund his gambits any longer, and he found himself penniless. Characteristically undaunted, Ledyard decided to go to England in search of potentially wealthy relatives his grandfather (now deceased) had mentioned. He obtained passage by working as a sailor, but upon arrival at the English Ledyards' doorstep he was coldly turned away. It was 1774, and as a young man on the street he was soon impressed into the British navy. Opportunity beckoned, however, when he heard that the famous English explorer, Capt. James Cook—a former farm boy, now already a two-time circumnavigator of the globe—was outfitting for a third trip. Ledyard talked his way on to the crew and sailed off on the experience of a life-time.

Cook took two ships, the *Resolution* and the *Discovery*, both well stocked and outfitted in what has been called a floating labo-ratory. Cook's goal was to discover a passage across the top of North America via the north Pacific, inspired by Vitus Bering's earlier exploration there for Russia. The Spanish too had been up and down the Pacific coast. The area was of little value to Eu-rope—unless the fabled Northwest Passage hidden somewhere in the far north truly existed. The British crown offered a prize of twenty thousand pounds sterling to the first British commander to find such a passage, which would make global trade faster and safer—and under English control. No longer would English ships have to pass through Spanish waters if a northern passage were available. Such a passage would also decrease the risk of scurvy, the bane of sailors on lengthy voyages.

Upon returning to London, the crew's journals and papers were confiscated and held by the admiralty. They were to be ex-amined and returned after Cook's official version of events (and discoveries) was published. This was the usual practice, and the men "cheerfully complied"; Ledyard's precious journals were taken along with those of the other crew members.[4]

Ledyard spent the next two years in the British navy, and it is unclear what duties he was given. The colonies were in full re-volt, however, and he, along with anyone else available, was dis-patched to fight the uprising. In December 1782 he arrived at Long Island on a British man-of-war. The area was in possession of the British at the time, and Ledyard, dressed in his navy attire, went to visit his mother who resided nearby. He found her man-aging a boardinghouse for British officers, and he obtained a room there. One can imagine, with his penchant for dramatics, that he was delighted when she finally suspected something odd about the new boarder and recognized him as her son, gone eight years. Both played the parts, however, pretending not to know each other, and he slipped away to hide out at his uncle's home in Connecticut.

He promptly sought a Connecticut publisher for the memoir of his voyage with Cook, written from memory, and it was quickly published in June 1783 despite wartime paper shortages. The colonies had been at war with Britain for six years, and Ledyard's book made him a patriotic hero for sharing England's geographic, scientific, and political knowledge with Americans. Besides the adventurous journey taken with the famous Cook (who had been killed by natives in the Sandwich Islands) Ledyard's book revealed something extremely interesting to maritime New England readers. A hugely profitable new trade in Alaskan sea otter fur to China was discovered while Ledyard sailed with Cook in the north Pacific.

When Cook's ships first reached the Pacific Northwest, they had landed at an island known as Onalaska, where natives wearing blue linen shirts and trousers met them, eager to barter for rum, tobacco, or snuff. Ledyard wrote that "the most remarkable circumstance was a cake of rye meal newly baked, with a piece of salmon in it, seasoned with pepper and salt, which was brought and presented to Cook by a comely young chief." The European food was a clear sign that other Europeans were already somewhere nearby. Natives at this remote spot had clearly been trading with Europeans, but who?

Cook decided he could spare only one man to go ashore and investigate; one alone could move quicker than a large armed party, and the loss of one man would not be a critical loss to the trip. When Ledyard volunteered, Cook admonished him to return by the end of a week; the ship would remain only two weeks in the harbor, no longer, before departing. Following Cook's advice, Ledyard went ashore unarmed, carrying only bottles of brandy for Indian gifts and some bread to eat. He traveled with the chief and two other natives, and when they arrived at a village he "was surprised at the behavior of the Indians, for though they were curious to see me, yet they did not express that extraordinary curiosity, that would be expected had they never seen an European before. . . ." He realized that they were already quite familiar with Europeans, "and I was glad to perceive it, as it was an evidence in favor of what I wished to find true, namely, that there were Europeans now among them."[5] The natives took him in a covered skin canoe, the type with two holes for riders, but Ledyard had to ride on his back in the space between the paddlers, unable to see a thing for about an hour's trip. They arrived at a village of approximately thirty Russians where he spent a comfortable night, and in the morning he took a hot bath and breakfasted on whale, sea horse, and beans, all smoked or dried.[6] The Russians had been trading furs there for five years. Three Russians and the native escorts accompanied Ledyard back to rendezvous with Cook, and Ledyard later noted that "the satisfaction this discovery gave Cook, and the honor that redounded to me, may be easily imagined. . . ."[7]

Not only did Cook's crew discover that the Russians were trading in what had been considered Spanish domain, they learned why the Russians had been keeping it such a secret. While stopped at Nootka, a Russian-Spanish post on Vancouver Island, the crew picked up a load of furs which they needed on board as bedding in the cold north, particularly since Cook was determined to head nearer to the Arctic. Later, on the return to

England, the ships stopped in China and traded the furs (a year after bartering for them) in Canton for astounding prices.

The crew nearly mutinied in their eagerness to go back for more, but instead they returned to London, ending a voyage of four years and three months. The trip gained greater knowledge of the Pacific and its islands, but it was the news of the potential fur trade that was most exciting. Bartering otter furs for a pittance from eager natives, then turning them over profitably in China for silks and porcelain that yielded high prices at home, promised a tidy fortune. The potential for trade could not be ignored, and after publication of Ledyard's book in America, which appeared well before Cook's in England, the secret was no longer just Russian or British but American as well.

In spite of his intimate knowledge of the trade, Ledyard was unable to find backers to help him found a shipping enterprise on the Northwest coast.[8] The country was mired in a serious financial depression, particularly the coastal seaports, because of wartime economics.[9] There were few markets, and once the war ended, no longer were there British troops to supply. Ledyard headed to Spain, then on to France in search of financiers for a trip to the Pacific Northwest.

In Paris Ledyard met the famous American privateer John Paul Jones, in town to collect payment from the French government. Jones had captured British ships during the Revolution and had sent them to French ports where they were kept as prizes. Expecting to receive significant payment, and already fairly wealthy, Jones agreed to work with Ledyard. The two planned to establish a fur-trade fort on the Alaskan coast—Jones would do the seafaring, Ledyard the bartering and coastal exploring. They planned to take two ships and twenty men. The two risk-takers discovered soulmates in each other—Jones even gave Ledyard

money to begin buying cargo. But it took months for Jones to receive his payment from the French, and the amount was far less
than he anticipated. The two men then tried interesting the
French court in a government-backed venture under the French
flag, but that fizzled. Jones's enthusiasm for the hopeless project
waned, and plans eventually collapsed.

But Ledyard's friendship with Jones had given him entrée to
the higher levels of French society. Jones was a hero in France—
his statue was displayed at the king's library, and he had been
crowned with laurels three times at the Opera House in Paris.
Through Jones, Ledyard had become acquainted with the Marquis de Lafayette and others who now supported him while he
planned the next venture. Ledyard also met Benjamin Franklin,
the U.S. minister to France, as well as his replacement, Thomas
Jefferson. And he encountered several other penniless opportunists who lived as hangers-on, seeking financing from wealthy
patrons for a variety of adventures that only needed cash.[10]

Ledyard realized his chances for putting together a shipping
enterprise in the Pacific Northwest were nil, so he began to plan
the only alternative open to a penniless adventurer: seeking
"honest fame." He would travel overland to the Pacific. After all,
he had met Russians in the far north and imagined he could simply come to the Pacific coast via Siberia. Without a ship, or even
passage on one, he would go by land, and he would *walk*. He discussed his scheme with Thomas Jefferson, who enthusiastically
took it up.

Jefferson applied for official permission from the Russian
minister at the French court. Trying to fill beloved "Papa
Franklin's" shoes in France was a humbling task for Jefferson;
Ledyard's wild schemes gave Jefferson something to do, and he
busied himself with letters to Russian dignitaries as well as to

Lafayette. Jefferson wrote to the Frenchman in February 1786, describing Ledyard as the fellow "who proposes to undertake the journey through the Northern parts of Asia and America."[11] Jefferson was enamored with Ledyard, who was everything he was not: daring, adventurous, and well traveled. He described Ledyard as having "genius" and "ingenuity," but, as he wrote to friends, the intrepid adventurer "unfortunately has too much imagination."[12] Nevertheless, if Ledyard actually succeeded in the plan, Jefferson could bask in his reflected glory as a fellow countryman who showed Paris how things were done in the new United States. The man would be a cheaper version of Cook, a "circum-ambulator" of the globe, making the trek afoot. Ledyard already touted himself as an expert on "how to live on nothing a year," a style of life that was the opposite of Jefferson's. To the Virginian, who had scarcely traveled before going to France and had never even visited the western United States, the concept of such an endeavor was exhilarating.

Jefferson's self-importance was enhanced by his relationship with Ledyard, but it did little to help the explorer. Ledyard regretted the involvement by officials, which in fact delayed his departure. He wrote to his cousin, "You see that I have so many friends, that I cannot do just as I please."[13] He yearned to set out immediately in order to cross Siberia before winter, but because Jefferson had alerted the Empress Catherine of Russia with a formal petition for the journey, he was forced to await a response. He waited five months, impatient to be off and avoid diplomatic etiquette, writing to his cousin that he was running four miles a day in training while waiting to hear from the empress, whom he referred to as "Kate of the North."[14]

During the delay, Ledyard's earlier dream of sailing for furs revived. Some English merchants, under the direction of Sir

James Hall, had outfitted a ship, and now they invited Ledyard to join in a trip to the Alaskan coast. Although fur trading had been his original plan, he quickly changed his mind and decided to go to Alaska on Hall's ship, then disembark and trek across North America overland. Elated, he bought two dogs, an Indian pipe, and a hatchet—his equipment for the overland portion of his trip. While it seems unlikely outfitting for a cross-continent journey across North America, it made sense. The dogs would provide protection for a lone traveler and help with hunting; the pipe would help establish friendship with Indians; the hatchet would ensure his survival. His biographer Jared Sparks, writing in 1828, agreed that Ledyard could not have selected "three more essential requisites for a solitary traveler among savages and wild beasts."[15]

Ledyard estimated it would take him three years to travel overland from Nootka to Virginia. The endeavor promised to provide information on geography and natural history as well as capture a measure of fame for Ledyard, which he could parlay into a career of some sort. "There was a romantic daring in the enterprise itself," Sparks points out, which was "well suited to gain the applause of ardent and liberal minds."[16] Ledyard knew the interests of European and American elites ran to scientific discovery, and, like Cook, he looked to gain whatever financial prize a significant discovery might yield.

While waiting in London for Hall's ship to be readied, Ledyard became close friends with Col. William Smith, on John Adams's staff. Adams was the U.S. minister to Britain, and Smith was married to his daughter. Ledyard shared his plans with Smith, who detailed them in a letter home to John Jay, then secretary of foreign affairs. "He means to attempt to march through the Indian nations to the back parts of the Atlantic states; for the purpose of examining the country and its inhabitants; and he expects to be able to make his way through, possessed of such information of the country and people, as will be of great advantage to ours. . . . It is a daring, wild attempt. . . . If he succeeds, and in the course of two or three years should visit our country by this amazing circuit, he may bring with him some interesting information. If he fails, and is never heard of more, which I think most probable, there is no harm done." Smith added a guarded warning: "It may not be improper for your excellency to be acquainted with these circumstances, and you are the best judge of the propriety of extending them further."[17] The letter was written to Jay on September 1; by the end of the following month, Hall's ship had been pulled back into port and held by customs just as it got under way. Whether Jay or Adams put a halt to the mission is unknown.

Ledyard's hopes for the voyage vanished, but he quickly turned his attention to his earlier alternative plan. To his uncle in Connecticut he wrote, "I am going in a few days to make the tour of the globe from London east on foot." He let Jefferson and others in France know of his change in plans and his lack of funds. Sparks believed Ledyard would have gone anyway this time, money or not. "He had lived too long by expedients to be stopped in his career, by an obstacle so trifling in his imagination as the want of money, and he was panting to get into a country, where its use was unknown, and where of course the want of it would not be felt."[18]

Ledyard began an overland trek by way of St. Petersburg, where he expected to be given official permission to enter Russia as a traveler. He left that city in June 1787, going on foot or riding with other travelers. Eventually Catherine rejected Ledyard's idea, calling it "chimerical." Jefferson wrote to Ledyard, telling him of Russia's refusal to support his effort to cross Asia, but hoping his plan would nonetheless find success.[19] Ledyard, without funds or escorts, or the official government assistance he had hoped for, set out alone.

He was treated well, wining and dining with governors and military officers, and wrote letters home to friends and supporters. He spoke French during the trip and at various times passed himself off as a special courier, a madman, or a student of natural history. His flair for drama allowed him easily to adopt whatever persona he needed. He enjoyed being the center of attention in Siberia, where he wrote to Jefferson that he was the first American the people had seen—"Those who have heard of America flock round to see me." But his tattooed hands, a souvenir of Polynesia with Cook, gave the Russians the wrong impression. "Unfortunately the marks on my hands procures me and my Countrymen the appellation of wild men."[20]

Jefferson supplied Ledyard with money—probably from his own funds—over the next few years. The traveler continued to write bread-and-butter letters to his patron, noting the items that interested Jefferson, such as the racial makeup of people he met, the physical features of people and landforms, and now and then mentioning a mammoth bone or two. Racial distribution was important because no one knew for certain whether North America and Asia were connected by a land link in the Arctic. The similarity in appearance and customs between Asians and North American Indians lent credence to the idea that the continents were joined, and would have disproved the possibility of a Northwest Passage.

But it was not an easy trip, and Ledyard was somewhat disappointed with the advice that others had given him before the undertaking. He was surprised at the difficulty he encountered during the trip, writing to William Smith that their discussions about Russia had been wrong: "You and I were extremely uninformed," Ledyard admitted. Travel by foot was nearly impossible, roads were impassable come autumn, and it was not a trip easily made without cash. "As for going on foot, it is ridiculous in this country," he wrote. If he missed the season's last mail wagon, he planned to rent a sled pulled by dogs or reindeer.[21] Both Jefferson and Ledyard believed that a lone traveler was less likely to be a target for robbery or murder if he carried little baggage. Equipment, papers, and weapons would only draw unwanted attention.

Jefferson had devised a unique means for Ledyard to identify longitude on his trek. He advised Ledyard to have a twelve-inch mark tattooed onto his arm. From that he was to measure latitude by using a stick and the shadow cast from the sun.[22] According to Capt. Nathanial Cutting of Boston, Jefferson had told Ledyard how to use the tattoo to find the latitude of his location: "He was to form a circle on the surface of the Earth, then placing a strait stick perpendicular in center, observe where the shadow came to at Sunrise and where it struck at Sunset, then dividing this distance on the Periphery would give the Point where the shadow ought to strike at noon:—having thus discover'd the sun's Southing, he was to break a strait stick just to the measure of a Foot which was mark'd on his arm and when he perceiv'd the Sun on the meridian he was to place this stick in a perpendicular position, and mark the length of the shadow which it Cast. This he was to record upon his skin. . . ." After Cutting told this story to John Adams, Adams wrote in his own diary that had Ledyard "pursued his north-west road, whatever benefit his success might have procured to mankind, his journal upon his skin would not, I think, have been worth much."[23]

In Siberia Ledyard met up with Capt. Billings, who was exploring the far reaches of Russia's Siberian coast for the Empress Catherine. While visiting Billings, Ledyard was delayed by officials who advised him against proceeding farther because of the weather, and shortly afterward, in January 1788, he was arrested at Irkutsk. Theories abound about why Ledyard was stopped and arrested; some Russians suspected he was a French spy, but most likely he was intercepted because Russian fur traders did not want him going farther. Efforts to establish a solid base of fur-trading establishments along the coast had been intensifying in the preceding two years.[24] The Russians probably had no knowledge that Ledyard had been to Nootka on Cook's ship, and had already seen firsthand the profitable yet secret trade going on between the Russian traders at Nootka and Canton.

Under Catherine's orders, Ledyard was arrested and returned unceremoniously to Moscow for interrogation, then dumped across the border in Poland with a warning never to return to Russia. He had traveled nearly across the continent, going alone and unencumbered, like Marco Polo. He had traveled on foot, by river bateau, by ox-drawn sledge over ice, and on horseback with Mongolian tribesmen. Yet the adventure was only that—no honor or prestige accrued from his efforts.

In Poland Ledyard borrowed money to get to London, where he was quickly recruited for an exploring venture in Africa. Under the auspices of the Society for the Promotion and Discovery of the Interior Parts of Africa and its two hundred financial supporters, he set out to find the origin of the Niger River. He did not get past Cairo, however, where he was detained for months trying to make connections with a caravan that would take him to the interior. Jefferson kept tabs on the adventurer, writing to American friends in July 1788 about Ledyard's Russian experience and his African venture, adding, "He promises me, if he escapes through this journey, he will go to Kentuckey and endeavor to penetrate Westwardly from thence to the South Sea."

In November 1788 Ledyard wrote to Jefferson after having spent three months in Cairo. He was ready to leave with a slave caravan in two or three days. Egypt, he wrote, was not at all as Jefferson had imagined; he should burn his books that romanticized travel there. "I think most historians have written more to satisfy themselves than to benefit others," Ledyard wrote. "I am certainly very angry with those who have written of the countries where I have traveled, and of this particularly. They have all more or less deceived me. In some cases perhaps it is difficult to determine, which does the most mischief, the self love of the historian, or the curiosity of the reader; but both together have led us into errors, that it is too late now to rectify." He complained that "I have passed my time disagreeably here," noting that treatment received by Christians was "humiliating," and calling the residents "a banditti of ignorant fanatics."

Ledyard died unexpectedly in Cairo a few days after the letter was mailed, at the end of November 1788. He was thirty-seven years old.[25] He was said to have taken a strong emetic (which may have been poison) which caused excessive vomiting, a broken blood vessel, and death in less than a week, according to a Mr. Hunter, an English merchant who had been traveling with him. Months before Jefferson learned of his friend's death, he wrote to a friend that Ledyard would "probably never emerge again" from the African adventure.[26] While some accounts claim that Ledyard committed suicide, it is just as likely that a traveling companion may have robbed and murdered him.

IN SPITE OF their opportunities, American merchants were slow to enter the Arctic fur trade. After all, the country had just risen from the ashes of a revolution, financial depression plagued commercial interests, and financing a long-distance trip with no certain outcome was difficult at best. But why was Britain too so dilatory in entering the fur trade in the Pacific Northwest? After all, it was Cook who had stumbled onto the market in the first place. Arctic furs solved the problem of what to haul into Canton in order to return with holds filled with silks and spices. Otter fur bought for pennies on the Nootka coast could be sold for one hundred dollars in China—the potential for profit was huge.[27] But British traders, while aggressively competing with other nations, were not allowed to compete among themselves. The crown granted licenses for protected territories, limiting where and what a company could trade and transport. The South Sea Company and the East India Company were separate business entities, and the sea otter furs were located in the territory of one company while the Canton market was within the trade territory of the other. No other British traders were allowed to enter the restricted trading realm. The New England traders, however, were limited only by their ability to finance the voyage, which was exactly what John Ledyard had come up against.[28] Eventually they made fortunes.

HISTORIANS have had a hard time determining whether Jefferson or Ledyard conceived the plan to cross North America from the West. Writing in 1813, Jefferson claimed it was his idea, but a letter Ledyard wrote in 1786 to Jefferson declared that he had planned the trip a year earlier. It is clear, however, that Jefferson was a friend, encourager, and financial supporter.[29]

While Ledyard did not succeed in his quest to explore North America from the West, he did have a lasting impact on history. "That he finally accomplished little, compared with the magnitude of his designs, was his misfortune, but not his fault," Jared Sparks wrote.[30] He made this judgment in 1828, years before the magnitude of the American West and the nation's inevitable spread from shore to shore could even be imagined. Ledyard's efforts were insignificant to the public, certainly, but he had had remarkable influence on one individual who mattered: Thomas Jefferson.

3

The French Botanist, the Fading War Hero, and Dreams of Empire

In order to make your representations more effective [you are] to direct opinion by means of anonymous publications. The Boston and Baltimore gazettes will be the best ones to use for distributing such publications in order to turn aside suspicion of authorship from you; but the more you contrive to influence public opinion indirectly, the more your official discussions with the President and with the Senate must be kept secret. . . . Your mission requires of you the greatest astuteness, but in order to be effective it must be secret.—The French government's instructions to Edmond Genet, 1793[1]

GEORGE ROGERS CLARK was a frontier fighter who led the revolutionary struggle in the West. He defeated the British and their Indian allies in the Illinois country and became the most popular postwar political figure in the Western region.

After the war he settled into frontier life, struggling to pay debts and make a living. His little brother, William, who would later head west with Meriwether Lewis, was only thirteen years old when, in December 1783, George received an interesting proposition from Thomas Jefferson. Clark had sent Jefferson some shells and seeds, and was continuing to watch for fossil bones, teeth, or tusks of the elusive "mammoth" that Jefferson hoped existed somewhere in America. Jefferson may have been influenced by the publication of John Ledyard's book when he wrote to Clark that a "very large sum of money" had been raised in England for "exploring the country from the Mississippi to California. They pretend it is only to promote knoledge [sic]. I am afraid they have thought of colonizing into that quarter. Some of us have been talking here in a feeble way of making the attempt to search that country. But I doubt whether we have enough of that kind of spirit to raise the money. How would you like to lead such a party?"[2] Clark declined the lackluster offer, claiming he had too many debts to pay after investing personal funds in fighting the Revolution. He was nearly bankrupt and anxiously awaiting repayment from the State of Virginia.[3] Someone else would have to compete against the English.

Less than five years after Jefferson queried him about exploring west to the Pacific, George Rogers Clark had begun to work for Spain in return for a liberal land grant. Virginia would not repay his war debts and his future as a businessman-farmer in Kentucky appeared brightest if he were linked with the more prosperous Spain. "Clark was disgusted with the neglect which Virginia and the United States gave to his claims," explains the historian Frederick Jackson Turner.[4] Twenty-nine-year-old Gen. James Wilkinson, another Revolutionary War veteran turned merchant and politician in Kentucky, also had begun working for

Spain, receiving money for his efforts to separate Kentucky from the Union.[5] Even though Spain was paying these and many other individuals, their earlier military efforts on the frontier made them dangerous to Spanish interests should the budding United States push its boundaries farther. Their loyalties could never be completely trusted, but as informants they were invaluable to Spain.

Another war veteran, the physician James O'Fallon, hatched his own plans to seek opportunity via Spain. In 1788 he wrote to Diego de Gardoqui, a Spanish official in New York, a long letter detailing his ambitious scheme to colonize the northern region of East Florida. He was an Irishman and pointed out that Spain had two threats to the Floridas: the United States and England. His proposition would negate both. He sought financing from Spain in efforts to settle 5,000 families on 857 acres of land each along the border of East Florida. All would be Catholic and predominantly Irish.[6] He assured the Spanish that the colony would only appear to be independent—the residents would actually be "the slaves of Spain, under the appearance of a free and independent colony."[7] The Spanish response was to wait and watch this "restless and turbulent adventurer."

Many "adventurer-colonists" were trying to barter with Spain in what must have been a flurry of letters and petitions to amaze Spanish officials. James Wilkinson himself had ignited most of the activity after he visited New Orleans in 1787 and began plying his services to Madrid. There were so many eager players, they began to step on one another's toes. Wilkinson intercepted a letter that O'Fallon wrote to Spanish officials, and discovered that O'Fallon and Clark intended to settle in the very region he and his Kentucky followers had planned to move in on, some Choctaw land in the Yazoo country. Wilkinson incorporated himself into the enterprise and funneled information to Spanish officials. The information startled the Spanish governor at New Orleans, Estevan Miro, who wrote to Wilkinson that the land they focused on was Indian land and could not be given up to anyone; it was also well within Spanish territory. Any attempt by the Americans to set up a colony would be resisted with force.[8]

The idea of force only encouraged O'Fallon and Clark. In the summer of 1790 they set about making military preparations to move ahead against Spanish resistance. They had signed on between three thousand and five thousand armed men in the Carolinas and Georgia, and more from Kentucky. After gathering, they planned to boat down the Tennessee, Ohio, and Mississippi rivers, meeting at the Yazoo River. They would be ready to fight, organized in companies of one hundred men each and under rigid military discipline. Besides the militia, plans included a force of three cavalry companies and four hundred infantrymen. "Female adventurers . . . married or marriageable" were invited to participate; each would receive a hundred acres in the colony. The first woman to arrive would get five hundred acres, the first to bear a child, "bastard or legitimate," in the new settlement would also get five hundred acres.[9] There would be something for nearly everyone.

By November 1790 O'Fallon was ready to move and had received word from Philip Nolan, a spy working for Wilkinson, that the time was right. No opposition would be made to the settlement by either Spaniards or Indians. Plans were for three hundred men to set out, with three hundred more troops to follow; six hundred families would go downriver in February. In November O'Fallon advertised the colony in Kentucky newspapers, describing the fine soil and agricultural potential as well as the substantial military force to protect the colonists. General

East Florida in 1803

Wilkinson would follow with one thousand fighting men in December, and another matching force would go as well. Thousands of people were involved.

Had the scheme succeeded, it might have rewritten the history of the American West. But men who hatch plans like this often get caught up in their own greed, opportunism, and dishonesty, and Wilkinson and O'Fallon were each other's match. Internal plotting and Wilkinson's continued filtering of information to the Spaniards for pay undermined the whole effort.

While Wilkinson was describing the plans to the Spanish, O'Fallon had been writing thirty-page letters to President Washington. The president had issued a proclamation in August 1790, warning that Indian treaties and regulations must be honored. O'Fallon attempted to gain his support, or at least consent, for the colony. In a letter to Washington, without naming names, he told of Wilkinson's plans to separate Kentucky from the Union as well as Wilkinson's close communications with Spanish officials. O'Fallon presented Washington with the opportunity to hire himself as a secret agent and spy for the United States.[10] Washington did not respond.

As the relationship between Wilkinson and O'Fallon shriveled, O'Fallon built a friendship with George Rogers Clark, enlisting Clark to lead the troops in the venture. This shift from Wilkinson to Clark accompanied a shift in O'Fallon's vision: working peacefully with Spain looked less likely, so he threatened to move on Florida in force, looking to England or the United States as allies. Even the Indians might be a better ally than Spain.

The Chocktaw and Chickasaw tribes were integral to the new colony's success. If they chose to fight, there was no way the Americans could settle. If Spain chose to incite the Indians against the Americans, any plans to establish a colony would be futile. Letters from O'Fallon to Spanish officials were thus peppered with requests, even pleadings and threats, to help control the Indians. There were thousands of emigrants waiting along the Atlantic coast, he boasted, but they could not move south until Indian hostilities were ruled out. As months dragged on into 1791, the most O'Fallon accomplished was to marry George Rogers Clark's younger sister, Frances. Now a brother-in-law to the general, O'Fallon's problems only multiplied.

As O'Fallon's political intrigues worsened, Wilkinson sought to drive him out of the country, possibly fearing that O'Fallon's disclosures might ruin his career. Wilkinson undermined the operation, accusing O'Fallon of misusing funds, and the grandiose scheme began to fade. Writing to Philip Nolan in February 1791, Wilkinson explained, "O'Fallon . . . has engaged General Clark to command his troops, and has made extensive contracts for provisions, Negroes, horses, etc. The company offered me 20,000 acres as a compliment, but I finally rejected it."[11]

The colony was hopelessly mired in debt, had made enemies all around, and faced increased opposition from the Spanish, who had built up fortifications below the mouth of the Yazoo River, at the very point where the colony would be situated. Things changed, however, when political alliances shifted and war between France and Spain appeared imminent. This energized O'Fallon and Clark, who plotted a new venture for themselves and hundreds of unhappy frontier families. Around Christmastime in 1792, they developed a scheme to attack Louisiana under the French flag—if the money arrived.

The French Revolution had occurred just before Thomas Jefferson returned to the United States in 1789. Following the startling success of the Republic, French political leaders touted plans to extend their revolution to all regions of the world still under monarchy. That meant the western portion of North America, where Spain still held the reins, and Canada, which was under England's control. Hearing that American settlers had plans and leaders already in place reinforced ideas that had been circulating in Paris to foment an attack on Spanish holdings. The French government dispatched to the United States a new ambassador, Edmund Genet, who was to circulate, gain support, and enlist the American government in working with its longtime ally France.

The French effort to seize North America was an aftershock

of the French Revolution, and one scarcely noticed by historians. Frederick Jackson Turner writes: "One of the gravest dangers of this period has not received the attention which its importance warrants." Genet was not simply an eccentric traveler acting as a rabble-rouser; the most important feature of his mission was "the desire of the French Republic to form connections with the frontiersmen of America and to seize Louisiana, the Floridas and Canada as a part of the same enthusiastic crusade for liberty that carried the French armies across the European frontiers in the early days of the Revolution."[12] French plans, however, required the support of the American people, especially the frontiersmen who had become distanced and unhappy with the national government, weak as it was.

IN 1793 the French National Assembly voted to try the king for treason, found him guilty, and sent him to the guillotine a week later. Ten days later France declared war on Britain. French and British sympathies extended to the former colonies, where citizens fell along two lines—those who still held a Tory-like nostalgia for Britain, and those who saw the French as allies in the American Revolution and partners for overthrowing monarchies. Mobs gathered, marched, and rioted in Charleston, Philadelphia, and New York. By the late spring of 1793, what had begun as lively debates deteriorated into brawls and riots in the major cities. At issue was whether America should enter the war—not a popular idea with government officials. The French, however, were eager to enlist Americans, because that meant Spain and England would have to fight on two fronts—in both Europe and North America—once again.

Since the start of the French Revolution, plans had been afloat to coordinate a similar revolution in Louisiana. A series of proposals appeared in Paris by 1792, all relying on the assistance of American and French settlers along the Ohio, Tennessee, and Cumberland rivers. Among those who presented proposals to the French government were a poet, a writer, a Princeton graduate who had served as sheriff in London, as associate of Benjamin Franklin, and a few mercenaries, as well as George Rogers Clark, whose proposal was presented by Thomas Paine in Paris.[13] The prize for the organizer, if indeed one were selected and backed by France, was to be a swath of public lands and commercial advantages.

A flurry of French agents now entered the United States to infiltrate the network of Democratic Clubs which the Jeffersonians had organized as a party effort to carry them into the presidency. To the eleven clubs which existed in early 1793, two dozen more were added within months. French agents were members of them all, and they began to foment an uprising. Noah Webster saw it all firsthand, criticizing the French efforts in newspaper articles. He realized that the French were "gradually and secretly" building strength until they could publicly defy the government and the Constitution. He noted that "in 1793 I was persuaded of its fatal tendency, and set myself to unmask the views of the founders of private clubs and to expose their dangerous effect on my unsuspecting fellow countrymen."[14] Webster described the French plans as "the most daring projects of throwing the world into confusion that have been exhibited since the incursions of the Goths and Vandals."[15]

The French government had considered sending Francisco de Miranda, a South American revolutionary, along with thirty thousand troops from Santo Domingo, in a brash effort to attack Spanish holdings in America. Miranda had been lobbying in Britain for support for a revolutionary effort he planned to spearhead—to take New Orleans, then conquer Mexico and South America. British officials had begun preparations to support Miranda's plan but had abandoned the idea in 1790 when it was ultimately determined to be impractical to march troops from New Orleans to Mexico. England wanted the Floridas and New Orleans, and though Mexico might be brought along as a dependency, the British had no desire for the rest of Louisiana, except as a bargaining chip to open commercial opportunities elsewhere in the Spanish empire. England's interest in Miranda's plan was based on commercial opportunity, not a desire to help in freeing Spanish colonists from their oppressors.[16]

Instead of Miranda, the French sent Genet, who had just been thrown out of Russia where Catherine discovered he was organizing Jacobin clubs in St. Petersburg.[17] His next assignment was the United States, where he was instructed to use the press to print anonymous articles to shape public opinion for an insurrection. He was to operate as a one-man public relations firm, salting the newspapers with propaganda.

Arriving first in South Carolina, Genet found himself quite fortunately at the center of wildly secessionist turmoil. The locals already hated the federal government, and in the Carolinas a popular majority had opposed the Constitution and the establishment of a strong federal government.[18] The enterprising Frenchman could not have found a more ready and willing audience; crowds burst into cheers and choruses of the "Marseillaise" after his fiery speeches. Genet traveled about the region, his frontmen scurrying ahead to print newspaper articles, fire up crowds, and distribute gallons of free rum.[19]

SIX YEARS after proposing his plan for western exploration to George Rogers Clark, Jefferson had returned from his stint as the U.S. foreign minister in France. He had left Paris in October 1789, just months after the beginning of the French Revolution. Upon his return he was appointed secretary of state in George Washington's cabinet. He had not sought the position and in fact hesitated before accepting it. He was uncomfortable with Washington—they held different views on many issues—and Jefferson nurtured a vision of himself as president one day. In the midst of the chaos provoked by Genet's activities, Jefferson astutely used the polarized politics to begin grooming support for his bid for the presidency in 1796. He "deliberately courted the Gallomaniacs,"[20] exploiting his connections to France.

Capitalizing on pro-French feelings, Jefferson defended and supported Genet, claiming his mission was "affectionate" and "magnanimous." Pro-Jefferson newspapers fueled the frenzy, with accusations that Hamilton, Adams, and Washington were plotting to establish a hereditary monarchy. Papers accused John Adams of subversion, and tasteless cartoons derided the elected leaders—with the exception of Jefferson, who was viewed as a French sympathizer.

Washington recognized that Americans in the South and West were unhappy. Southerners wanted less federal control but at the same time clamored for protection from Spanish-backed Indians in Georgia and along southern borders. In the West the federal government did not seem so valuable or important to those who fought their own battles with Indians and had no market for their wheat or livestock. Western settlements might just as easily align themselves with Spain, who exerted light control over Louisiana residents but carefully restricted American shipping on the Mississippi River. Farmers on the Western frontier had to rely on river transport in marketing their produce, making the Mississippi crucial. To prevent Western settlements from simply seceding—of which they were entirely capable—Washington astutely appointed influential Westerners to important government posts, essentially rewarding them for their loyalty.

As secretary of state, Jefferson was warned about Genet's plans before the French ambassador left Paris. His informant was William Smith, Ledyard's old friend and John and Abigail Adams's son-in-law. Smith told Jefferson that France was sending Genet to start an attack that would begin at the mouth of the Mississippi River and sweep southward along the Gulf of Mexico, and that France would have no objections if the United States took the Floridas as a prize.[21] France had expansive goals for North America; in one swoop it could meld the military campaigns of Europe, the discontented frontiersmen in the Mississippi Valley, and the revolutionary unrest that was brewing in all of Spanish America. "The historical possibilities of the great design are overwhelming," Frederick Jackson Turner notes.[22] If France, linked with American backwoodsmen, had been able to pull it off, North and South America would have been "liberated" and probably speaking French right now.

AMONG THE BEVY of French agents scattered across the new nation, one—André Michaux—spent more than a decade exploring, botanizing, and reporting on the conditions in the emerging nation. Michaux had been born in France, his father the superintendent of the royal estate. Young Michaux had been destined to do the same. Schooled in classical studies, agriculture, and botany, he would have been running the agricultural operations at the royal farms of Versailles if not for the upheaval in French politics. Intrigue interested him as much as botany, and he began traveling to seek out strange plants while documenting politics in England, the Pyrenees, and Persia. In 1785 the French govern-

ment sent him to North America to study the potential for trans-
planting forest trees to France. That assignment was an excellent
cover, allowing him to traverse the Allegheny Mountains and
journey north to Canada, both areas of intense political interest
to France. He tramped the Carolina backcountry, the Floridas,
and even the Bahamas, looking for commercially viable plants
such as ginseng, all the while jotting down useful information.
Michaux's diary documents the distances between settlements,
number and types of residents, landforms such as rivers and
mountains, and other information vital to military planning. He
dropped hints of names and meetings along the way, revealing
both his political astuteness and discretion. The historian Reuben
Thwaites modestly describes his activities by saying that "other
motives may have led him to this country under feint of herboriz-
ing." Like Genet, Michaux was a spy, and a busy one.

In 1791 Michaux, already famous for his botanical discoveries, suggested that the American Philosophical Society in
Philadelphia send him to explore the West via the Missouri
River, to gather information about natural science. He proposed
to make the trip overland. Jefferson, president of the Society in
1793, gathered donations from other members and created formal instructions for Michaux, to make sure that the funds were
well earned. Michaux would be paid in increments at specific
points as the journey progressed. Jefferson's written instructions
in April 1793 told Michaux what information the donors expected him to gather, while providing directions to pass north of
Spanish settlements to avoid being stopped. Certainly a French
citizen, in the employ of the United States, would be most un-
welcome in New Spain.

Interestingly, the instructions Jefferson drew up for
Michaux—which would be the basis for similar ones given to

Meriwether Lewis a few years later—appear to have been very similar to those Peter the Great drew up for Vitus Bering (1681–1741) to follow in 1728 as he explored the Aleutian Islands, what is now the Bering Sea, and the northeast coast of Siberia. The tsar's instructions to Bering were copied by Empress Catherine when she sent Capt. Joseph Billings on the expedition to Siberia, where in 1786 he encountered John Ledyard. No doubt Jefferson had read accounts of these expeditions and used the instructions as his model for American expeditions to the West.[23]

Michaux was almost ready to depart for the Missouri River when Genet arrived in Charleston in February 1793. Genet expected to negotiate secret U.S. government support for his plan while inflaming the populace in a huge public relations program. Believing he had Secretary of State Jefferson's approval, Genet began organizing a force of American volunteers.[24] He optimistically approached Treasury Secretary Alexander Hamilton for money to finance a militia in the West. Hamilton refused. When news surfaced about Genet's activities, citizens became polarized. The capital, Philadelphia, was in crisis.

Washington was furious; Genet's actions might be the excuse for Britain to declare war on the young nation, which would be unable to survive. And France would be dangerous even as an ally, ready to take the nation for itself once Spain was out of the picture. Washington held firm, issuing a declaration of neutrality requiring friendly and peaceful conduct toward foreign powers—anyone "aiding or abetting hostilities" or participating in non-neutral activities in the United States would be dealt with. There would be no wilderness armies attacking Spain. Many other elected officials agreed with Washington; Jefferson went along with the president's policy but did not agree. In a letter to James

Madison he called the proclamation "pusillanimity," noting that Genet had won huge popular support. "It is impossible for anything to be more affectionate, more magnanimous than the purport of his mission. . . . In short he offers everything and asks nothing," Jefferson told Madison.[25]

Denied help from the government, Genet turned to the public, setting off near anarchy, with riots in the streets and mobs generated by his agents.[26] When Genet arrived in Philadelphia, advance men rallied a thousand people in the streets each day he was there. Mobs threatened to drag President Washington into the streets and begin a revolution with France against Britain. Washington met with Genet and stressed his policy of neutrality. Genet ignored him and outfitted eight U.S. ships to act as French privateers. Washington ordered them out of U.S. waters—but with no navy to enforce his order, the command was useless.[27]

When he arrived in Philadelphia, Genet found a letter from George Rogers Clark, which told of his experience in the military, his investigations into Spanish strength in the Mississippi Valley, his many friends in the region, and his relations with the Indians. After this resumé, Clark offered to lead a force of four hundred men to expel the Spanish from Louisiana. He needed only two or three frigates and three thousand pounds sterling to get things under way.[28] Clark was by now a debt-ridden alcoholic, dragging up his past as an Indian fighter. "Crushed by debt and drink, Clark lusted desperately for the booty that would be his if he and his rag-tag mercenaries raised the French flag in Spanish-held Louisiana and the Floridas," explains the historian Harlow Unger.[29]

Genet received letters from André Michaux as well, who had been hired six months earlier to undertake the transcontinental exploration tour for Thomas Jefferson and the American Philosophical Society. Michaux's tour offered a superb cover for Genet's plans; Genet sent Michaux to meet with Clark and other potential collaborators in Kentucky, on what were ostensibly botanizing trips.

Elated over the prospects for success, Genet reported to France in June 1793 that events were in motion, that he enjoyed a wealth of popular support, and that he might be able to persuade Congress to meet and vote favorably to override "Old Washington." He was also having supplies sent to a base of operations in the Antilles and was "exciting the Canadians, arming the Kentuckians, and preparing an expedition by sea to assist with the attack on New Orleans."[30] It had been a busy month.

In the midst of the Terror in France, Genet continued his frenzied campaign, exhorting Philadelphia crowds to join the "Revolution of the World." Jefferson's Democrats used the situation to accuse Washington, Hamilton, and Vice President John Adams of plotting a monarchy, with Washington as king. Antigovernment newspapers printed incendiary articles and cartoons. Noah Webster, having dined at the same hotel table with Genet, later reported that when he chastised the Frenchman for calling Washington and his administration fools, Genet shot back, "Mr. Jefferson is no fool."[31] Indeed Jefferson was never a fool. He quickly distanced himself from Genet, accusing him of being "hotheaded." Genet's actions placed Jefferson in an embarrassing position, and he submitted his resignation as secretary of state, to take effect at the close of 1793.[32]

In the end, the people were loyal to President Washington, the frontier was not handed to France, and Genet's popularity plummeted. As the Jacobins replaced the Girondin party in France, Genet no longer received support for his work, and attention turned to the fighting on France's own borders and the Reign of Terror in the streets. Liberating the Western Hemisphere no longer mattered quite as much. But Genet did not know that.

On July 5, 1793—ironically, the day after the nation's seventeenth anniversary—Genet met with Thomas Jefferson and disclosed in detail the plans to send a French fleet and fifteen hundred frontiersmen from Georgia and South Carolina to attack St. Augustine and liberate it from Spain. At the same time two thousand backwoodsmen would boat down the Tennessee River, joining George Rogers Clark and his forces. Genet told Jefferson about Michaux's instructions and read the draft of a speech he planned to deliver in Canada to incite Canadians to join the action.

Jefferson, knowing that Louisiana was the planned base of operations and that it would be declared independent from Spain, told Genet that "enticing officers and souldiers from Kentucky to go against Spain, was really putting a halter about their necks, for that they would assuredly be hung if they commenced hostilities against a nation at peace with the U.S." If Genet left the U.S. military out of it, enlisting only citizenry, that might be a different matter. "Leaving out that article [military personnel] I did not care what insurrections might be excited in Louisiana," Jefferson admitted. At the same meeting Jefferson wrote a letter of introduction for Michaux to Governor Isaac Shelby of Kentucky, and rewrote it under Genet's advice, adding that not only was Michaux "a man of science," he also had Genet's backing and support.

After meeting with Jefferson, Genet wrote to Paris that Jefferson had told him of the delicacy of political matters, because the U.S. government was negotiating with Spain to regain shipping privileges on the Mississippi River. "Nevertheless he made me understand that he thought that a little spontaneous irruption in New Orleans could advance the matter, and he put me into connection with several deputies of Kentucky and notably with Mr. Brown [a senator from Kentucky]."[33]

Meanwhile Michaux, with his journals, plant presses, and eye for detail, departed down the Ohio River in July 1793. While botanizing, he visited influential men in Kentucky to garner support for Genet's scheme. He visited George Rogers Clark at Clark's father's plantation in Mulberry Hill, near Louisville. There he delivered a provisional commission for Clark to act as commander-in-chief of the Independent and Revolutionary Army of the Mississippi, a belated response to Clark's earlier letter to Genet. "He told me that he was very eager for the Undertaking," Michaux noted, "but that, although he had written so long ago, he had rec'd no answer and thought it had been abandoned." Worse, Clark told Michaux that the plans in Kentucky had collapsed, "that a fresh circumstance seemed to oppose an obstacle to it."[34] Later that obstacle would be revealed in Spanish archives to have been the work of Gen. James Wilkinson, who had his own designs on the control of Western lands.

BY THE AUTUMN OF 1793 Genet found himself deserted by Jefferson. Jefferson had discovered that Genet did not offer something for nothing, and that France planned to embroil the United States in a war. He had warned Genet that summer not to communicate directly with the president, telling him that all correspondence from foreign diplomats must first pass through the secretary of state's office.[35] The Michaux expedition, which Jefferson had lauded publicly, was now an embarrassing revelation of his support for French undercover interests.

Soon the French government determined that Genet no longer served its purpose—he had alienated the United States government by stirring up the unruly masses. Washington's hostility had cost him popular American support as well. The Jacobins recalled Genet on March 6, 1794. The letter of recall arrived while Clark and friends were busy preparing to head down the Mississippi River for an assault on Spanish turf; troops were already in position along the Georgia frontier to attack St. Augustine. "Had the proclamation [recalling Genet] been delayed, the attempt would certainly have been begun," Frederick Jackson Turner writes. "What the result of such an attempt would have been, with the Spaniards fully informed, the military forces of the U.S. under orders to oppose it, and the leading friends of Genet already alienated . . ." is left to be imagined.[36]

George Rogers Clark could not believe the news; he had joined the wrong team. He had two thousand impatient men ready to move out, "declare them selves Citizens of France and Give freedom To their neibours on the Mississippi." He had munitions, men, a camp within fifty miles of the "Enemys Lines," and the popular support of everyone except the "arristocratical party." Everyone had been ready, "expecting Mr. Michaux with Supplies of money." But no word had come till the news arrived that the plan was being abandoned. Now Clark was faced with the task of breaking the news to others: "when the report of the failaur Shold reach the inhabitants of the Mississippi they will be miserable"—just as Clark was. He pointed out that his frugal war efforts had successfully forced Spain to spend $4 million in the preceding six months to reinforce against his efforts, which had cost him only a few thousand—that he hoped to recover. He begged France to reconsider: "the people in general yet Look up to them [France] for something to be Done as they are out of all acquired a wealth of botanical knowledge from his mother, who was a "yarb doctor," or practicing herbalist. Jefferson ignored the request at the time.

Lewis must have decided that if he could not take part in an exploring venture, at least he could do his patriotic duty. He joined the army as his father had, and went to fight the Whiskey Boys—disaffected frontiersmen like those Wilkinson and Clark had yearned to lead. William Clark, then in his early twenties, also joined the military, perhaps to escape the family farm where his alcoholic brother and mentally ill sister and her children might have made things far from easy. The only trait he seemed to share with his scurrilous older brother George was a propensity for poor spelling.

4

Wild Horses, Yellow Journalists, and a Lover of Glory

*. . . I look forward to the conquest of Mexico by the U.S.; and
I expect my patron and friend, the General, will, in such an
event, give me a conspicuous command.*
—Philip Nolan to Samuel Moore[1]

AN IRISH IMMIGRANT, Philip Nolan worked and lived
with James Wilkinson for four years from 1788 to 1791,
acting as his bookkeeper, clerk, and spy. Thomas Jefferson some-
how learned of Nolan while he worked for Wilkinson, and began
corresponding with him while Jefferson served as secretary of
state. In June 1790 Jefferson wrote to Nolan, "I have understood
that there are large herds of horses in a wild state, in the country
west of the Mississippi, and have been desirous in obtaining details of their history. . . . Mr. Brown, senator from Kentucky,

informs me it would be in your power to give interesting information on this subject, and encourages me to ask it." Jefferson had earlier introduced Edmund Genet to Senator Brown when Genet sought participants to initiate a rebellion in New Orleans.

While the wording of the letter to Nolan seems innocuous—it appears Jefferson is pursuing another eccentric notion, this time wild horses—the message behind the wording is as clear as Jefferson's equivocal language could be. He was encouraging Nolan to travel into Spanish territory and feed him with information. For example, in discussing the wild state of horses in North America, he notes that "I need not specify to you the particular facts asked for; as your knowledge of the animal in his domesticated, as well as his wild state, will naturally have led your attention to those particulars in the manners, habits, and laws of his existence, which are peculiar to his wild state. I wish you not to be anxious about the form of your information, the exactness of the substance alone is material; and if, after giving in a first letter all the facts you at present possess, you would be so good, on subsequent occasions, as to furnish others in addition, as you may acquire from time to time. Your communications will always be thankfully received, if addressed to me at Monticello, and put into any post office in Kentucky or Tennessee, they will reach me speedily and safely."[2]

When Daniel Clark, a New Orleans merchant who handled Nolan's mail, learned of Jefferson's interest, he warned the vice president to keep anything he learned from Nolan confidential. Any disclosure was dangerous to Nolan, who, Clark mysteriously said, "will all at times have it in his Power to render important Services to the U.S., and whom Nature seems to have formed for Enterprizes of which the rest of Mankind are incapable."[3]

Jefferson wrote to William Dunbar, a plantation owner at

Natchez, "We are not without hopes that Mr. Nolan may decide to try the Virginia market with his horses; in that case as my residence is on his best route, I may have the pleasure of seeing him personally and perhaps of purchasing one of his fine animals for the saddle, which I am told are so remarkable for the singularity & beauty of their colors & forms."[4] It is apparent that Jefferson sought to meet privately with Nolan. The horses were a cover, as horseflesh was highly esteemed and well bred in Virginia and Kentucky. F. A. Michaux, the French botanist's son, described mustangs similar to Nolan's in 1802: "These horses have a very unpleasant gait, are capricious, difficult to govern, and even frequently throw the rider and take flight."[5] Virginia horses, and definitely Jefferson's, were expensive saddle animals, selling for about $150 apiece.

It was not Nolan's rangy mustangs but his knowledge of the Spanish frontier that Jefferson wanted. An astute spy, Nolan became friendly with several Spanish officials and obtained a passport to enter the province of Texas. In 1791 he left Kentucky to take an illegal trade caravan into Texas, but his goods were confiscated. He remained in Texas without permission, living with Indians for two years before returning to New Orleans with 50 mustangs to sell. Because the Spanish soldiers badly needed cheap horses, they allowed him to go back—at the close of 1795 he returned with 250. After another trip to Texas, in 1799 he arrived in Natchez with 1,200 horses. The Spanish had become suspicious, however, because Nolan appeared to be stirring up the Texas Indians against Spanish rule. Their suspicions were confirmed when Spanish officials intercepted a letter from Nolan to a friend in Natchez: "Everyone thinks that I go to catch wild horses, but you know that I have long been tired of wild horses."[6] The Spanish governor of Natchez and Upper Louisiana, Gayoso de Lemos, reported Nolan to authorities as a dangerous man, a heretic, and a fraud. De Lemos warned that Nolan had only claimed to be interested in horses, all the while spying on the northern provinces of New Spain for General Wilkinson. The other officials heeded de Lemos's caveat, but the unfortunate governor died soon after a dinner party held for Wilkinson in New Orleans.[7]

Had he lived longer, Philip Nolan might well have been Jefferson's man to explore the West. Nolan was a "bold pathfinder, reckless mustanger, conniving entrepreneur, passionate adventurer, betrayed filibuster, and martyred freedom fighter."[8] After meeting with Jefferson he brazenly set out once more for Texas. Spanish posts along the border were alerted that Nolan was attempting to enter the territory with an armed force. He had gathered eighteen Americans, seven Spaniards, and two Negro slaves, all heavily armed and carrying sabers. Nolan himself carried a double-barreled shotgun, a pair of pistols, and a carbine. Outfitted like human arsenals, the group crossed into Spanish territory in early November 1800, in an expedition apparently eager to arouse the Spanish.[9]

Along the Brazos River near today's Waco, Texas, Nolan's men built three rough forts on Spanish land. They waited four or five months, trading with nearby Comanches. Meanwhile the Spanish turned out in force along the Rio Grande, in the largest military build-up to that time. The Spanish governors and commandants feared that the Americans and the British were about to move into Texas.[10] On March 21, 1801, the Spaniards found Nolan and his men ragged and starving, subsisting on horsemeat. A firefight ensued, killing Nolan, the only fatality. Some of his men escaped, others surrendered and were taken to prison.

Mystery still surrounds Nolan's venture. Why so many

armed men, and why did they settle down in a rough fort? What were they waiting for? And who was supporting them? Nolan certainly appeared to be part of a larger plot to invade Mexico. Was he waiting for a larger insurrection? Or waiting for word from Wilkinson or Jefferson to proceed with a plan? The historian Noel Loomis notes that "James Wilkinson was one of the crookedest men in history and one of the great opportunists. He was also very clever at covering his tracks on all sides." Nolan himself had written to a friend, "I look forward to the conquest of Mexico by the U.S.; and I expect my patron and friend, the General, will, in such an event, give me a conspicuous command."[11] Mordecai Richards, who had been one of Nolan's party but had deserted, claimed Nolan told the men they were to explore the country, round up horses, and wait for a group of volunteers in a scheme to invade and conquer Texas.[12]

Loomis points out that Nolan's hideout was in a strategic location and would have proven valuable if an army of Kentuckians had arrived. He knew the country well, and he knew the Spaniards were looking for him.[13]

Remaining letters from Nolan are few, and for good reason. When Nolan realized the Spanish suspected him as a spy, he stopped corresponding with Wilkinson, explaining that while he was in the West "a letter from a trader in horses to a General of the federal armies, would have confirmed suspicions that were nearly fatal to me." Letters to or from Thomas Jefferson would have been far more problematic.

IN APRIL 1793, the same month Edmund Genet arrived in Charleston, South Carolina, with plans to incite a revolution for France, a plucky Scottish journalist arrived in Philadelphia. James Callender had been forced to flee Scotland for his life after publishing the eighty-page pamphlet *Political Progress of Britain* in 1792, the same year George III outlawed seditious writings. Callender criticized British rule in Scotland and praised American colonists for revolting. By April 1793 a warrant had been issued for his arrest, and he slipped into hiding and onto a ship bound for Philadelphia.[14] This thirty-five-year-old educated man suddenly found himself without a country.

Callender settled in Philadelphia, where he was hired by Matthew Carey, a newspaper and magazine publisher who had worked for Benjamin Franklin in Paris.[15] Naturally Callender found Alexander Hamilton's pro-British views anathema, and found it natural to write for the Republicans. In 1797 he exposed Hamilton's affair with a married woman, Maria Reynolds, and accused him of mishandling government funds. For Hamilton the affair was not as damaging as the allegations of financial misconduct. He acknowledged his adultery but claimed it was a case of blackmail instigated by the woman and her husband. He had paid large sums of money to Mr. Reynolds, and as the secretary of the treasury his actions were suspect. His reputation was ruined; he never held public office again.

By 1798 Callender was writing for the *Philadelphia Aurora*, a newspaper run by Franklin's grandson Benjamin Bache. When the twenty-eight-year-old Bache was away from the *Aurora*, Callender took the reins.

For the Republicans and their leader, Thomas Jefferson, James Callender was made to order. Republican-financed newspapers were popping up all over the place, designed to use their power to influence the election of 1800. Jefferson had been defeated in 1796 in his first attempt for the presidency by John Adams, leader of the Federalist party, and thus settled for the vice presidency. Callender slung nasty slurs at political figures but also reminded his readers that John Adams had been one of the men who tried to unseat Washington as head of the army in 1777.

The battle of the presses ensued. In Philadelphia the *Gazette of the United States* attacked the *Aurora* and Callender, charging that "the Scotch renegade Callender is at present in the pay of [the *Aurora*] for the purpose of traducing the people of this country."[16] In March 1798 the *Gazette* again attacked Callender, this time as an "imported felon" and "a bitter enemy to the honor and independence of the United States."[17] That June the Federalists pushed the Alien Act through Congress, pointedly designed to control newly arrived immigrants like Callender (and Genet, busy farther south) who tried to stir up the masses. Between death threats, the death of Callender's wife, and caring for his four children, pursuing anti-Federalist journalism full-time under the meager salary at the *Aurora* no longer appealed to Callender.[18] He quickly became a legal citizen in order to avoid prosecution under the Alien Act but was arrested in August 1798 as he rode horseback outside of Leesburg, Virginia. He was charged with vagrancy but released after the Republican senator from Virginia became involved. Days later he was arrested and once again released after Republican politicians spoke on his behalf.[19]

The Federalists hated Callender, reacting strongly to his notoriously harsh pen. Described as "a little dirty toper with shaved head and greasy jacket, nankeen pantaloons and woolen stockings,"[20] he was considered a "wretch who boasted of having fled hither to escape the hands of justice . . . a runaway and incendiary, a vagabond, and a pauper."[21] At a time when only propertied men could cast votes, wage-earning immigrants like Callender were hard to accept in the political arena. In December 1798, the *Gazette of the United States* published a list of names of individuals who were scheming to generate another revolution. Callender's name was included along with other writers who worked for the *Aurora*.[22] A foretaste of the twentieth-century red hunts, the era reeked with turmoil over the limits of press freedom and the degrees of loyalty to be expected from citizens.

By June 1799 Callender was working as editor of a new Republican-supported newspaper, the *Richmond Examiner*. In August a plot to murder him was unmasked and stopped within hours.[23] With financial support from Jefferson, Callender tried his hand at book writing again and in February 1800 began distributing *The Prospect Before Us*. In its 184 pages he claimed that the country had been driven to a "dangerous juncture" with France by the "tardiness and timidity of Mr. Washington," which was "succeeded by the rancor and insolence of Mr. Adams." He railed that Adams, "the monarch of Massachusetts," was bound to pull the country into war with France.[24]

Jefferson was delighted with his investment, writing to Callender that the book would be highly effective, adding that "such papers cannot fail to produce the best effect." Although Jefferson would later try to distance himself from his "assistant writer," in light of his loss in 1796 he was determined to win in 1800 at any cost.

The Federalists had followed the Alien Act with a more flexible Sedition Act, making it a crime to attack the government or the president with slanderous or malicious accusations. In 1800, deep in the political propaganda campaign of an election year, Callender and several other newspaper writers were arrested, tried, and convicted under the act. Callender was charged with seditious libel of President Adams in *The Prospect Before Us* and received a $200 fine and a nine-month jail sentence.[25]

Undaunted, Callender accepted the situation, exploiting his

incarceration in the Richmond jail as he continued writing political tracts. With Jefferson's financial backing and encouragement, he published a second volume of *The Prospect Before Us*, a scathing political tract patterned after the earlier edition that had already landed him in trouble. He prefaced the book with comments about President Adams, "that scourge, that scorn, that outcast of America." His harangues of Hamilton and Adams alternated with ebullient pro-Jefferson statements, such as: "If you are desirous to live in peace and plenty, to keep your money for your own purposes, to see your barns full, your fences in repair, your cattle sleek, your slaves hearty and contented; if you are ambitious to be revered as a protector, and adored as a benefactor, to read, in the looks of your wife and children, the language of happiness, of gratitude, and of love; in a word, if you wish to taste of those delicious sympathies that sometimes prevent us from regretting this bitter tragedy of existence, then go, fly, and, as you value soul and body, vote for the Jefferson ticket!"[26]

He concluded the book by noting the many ways fraud and corruption were present in government, from theft by customs house agents to army contractors pinching the public's money. An early-day muckraker of sorts, Callender championed the press as a way to maintain what we might refer to today as "transparency" in government. "Corruption is one of the first elements of government," he admonished. "This again proves the necessity for an impartial and independent press; because government exists but by the support of public opinion, and the press is the axis around which public opinion may be said to revolve."[27]

James Callender cannot be ignored in any study of events related to Thomas Jefferson. He epitomizes the intrigue, backstabbing, and dirty politics of the era, as well as the power of the press to shape public opinion. If anyone realized the press's influence it was Jefferson, and he was adept at handling it—and those who drove it—with care.

Callender—called by some Jefferson's "hired writer"—expected that his work would pay off once the election was over. When Jefferson became president he did pardon Callender as well as the other incarcerated writers. But Callender was determined that Jefferson refund him the $200 libel fine, a substantial amount for a poorly paid writer. Jefferson, securely in the presidency, ignored Callender and began distancing himself from his former associate. Callender's work had been endorsed and financed by Jefferson for years—now, instead of a payoff, he was being put off.

The Scotsman informed Jefferson that he wanted a government appointment as postmaster for the city of Richmond. He is said to have loitered outside Jefferson's house for days in efforts to speak with the president. He shouted when he glimpsed the tall, red-haired Virginian at a window, "Sir, you know that by lying I made you President," then threatened to "tell the truth." Jefferson continued to ignore him, and asked James Monroe, governor of Virginia, to write statements that Jefferson had never paid Callender for his writing nor been involved in his salacious accusations against former President John Adams. Callender was no fool; he had saved the incriminating letters Jefferson sent him, and moved to make them public.

Callender was staying in a cheap boardinghouse in Washington City, where Jefferson sent his secretary, Meriwether Lewis, to pay Callender fifty dollars, ostensibly to cover part of his fine. Callender told Lewis he would blackmail Jefferson, telling the truth about their past dealings as well as other things that could "ruin" the president. After Lewis reported back to Jefferson, the president enlisted Monroe in an effort to retrieve any letters from Jefferson that Callender might still possess. Their efforts were unsuccessful.

To make his living while exacting revenge, Callender partnered with Henry Pace to print the *Richmond* (Virginia) *Recorder.* From his new post on the other side of the political fence, he threw accusations at Jefferson and his administration. The *Aurora* shot back at Callender with a vengeance, printing virulent personal attacks on its former writer. In 1802 Callender wrote that the nation would be better off if Jefferson had been beheaded five minutes before his inaugural speech—a swipe at both Jefferson and France. He also began printing articles about Jefferson's affair with Sally Hemings, a slave at Monticello. Callender claimed that Hemings went to France with Jefferson and his young daughter, not as a servant but as Jefferson's "wench." Callender claimed his story was based on fact, and that in Virginia "everybody believes it."[28]

The stories about Hemings boosted subscriptions to the paper, focusing critical attention on Jefferson. Sally Hemings was the unacknowledged half-sister of Jefferson's wife Martha, whose father had fathered Hemings with one of his slaves. Martha Jefferson inherited Hemings and several other slaves upon her father's death. Hemings eventually bore five children, and Callender insisted that Jefferson fathered them all. For nearly two centuries historians have debated whether the charges were accurate, until DNA testing in 1998 proved that Jefferson had indeed fathered at least one of Hemings's children.

Because Callender had already published Jefferson's letters incriminating him in financing his much-maligned *Prospect Before Us,* the public found Callender's assertions about Hemings credible, despite Jefferson's denials. As Jefferson biographer Joseph Ellis notes, Jefferson's character had been tainted with deception and denial, and "the duplicity that was exposed in his dealings with Callender was wholly in character."[29]

Along with the stories of the Hemings, Callender described an affair Jefferson had with a friend's wife and how he had tried to repay money he owed a friend with depreciated currency. All of these seriously harmful stories were true, and Callender claimed they were more than sensationalism. By insisting upon the importance of the public's examination of the moral character of its country's leaders, he was breaking new ground in politics. He used scandal and suspicion to provoke a critical estimate of powerful leaders during an era when the common man was beginning to insist on a stake in national government.

Meriwether Lewis, who had made at least one payment to Callender for Jefferson and who probably knew firsthand the truth behind the Sally stories, was in Pittsburgh that spring of 1803. He was ordering boats and supplies for his expedition west when Callender's body was found floating in three feet of water in the James River. The story was covered by local papers but ignored elsewhere—Lewis was probably completely unaware of it. The death was called accidental, likely resulting from intoxication. The *Richmond Examiner* claimed that Callender had committed suicide following the discovery of financial fraud perpetuated by his partner at the *Richmond Recorder.*[30] Later, when Jefferson tried to reconcile his friendship with John and Abigail Adams, denying his well-known, longtime involvement with Callender, Abigail rejected the overture. She told Jefferson that "the serpent you cherished and warmed, bit the hand that nourished him."[31] For Jefferson, explaining why he had ever been so involved for so long with Callender had become awkward. But now the man was forever silent.

Callender had emphasized how much one of Sally Hemings's children, a boy about ten or twelve years of age, resembled Jefferson. Said to have red hair and white skin (Hemings was described as appearing white herself), the child had even been named Tom. After the scandalous stories broke in the press, the child was no longer to be found at Monticello. As to whether he died, ran away, or was relocated or sold, no evidence has yet been found. Perhaps he never existed. Sally's two daughters were freed when they turned twenty-one; her sons Madison and Eston remained slaves at Monticello until they were manumitted at Jefferson's death. Hemings herself was freed by Jefferson's daughter a few years after Jefferson's death. Freeing Hemings would have been problematic for Jefferson during his lifetime—should he have chosen to do so—as he would have had to appeal to the Virginia legislature to let her remain in the state, which would have brought more attention to the situation.[32]

FOR JEFFERSON and his Republican followers, the vision of the future was a continent peopled with independent farmers who shared the same language, culture, and government ideals. Only two obstacles stood in the way: Spain, a fading power; and the Indians, who became more troublesome when they obtained rifles and horses. In Florida the Cherokees, Choctaws, and Seminoles were the bane of American settlers. Along the western bank of the Mississippi, more Indians who were equally loyal to Spain hindered Americans. Spanish governors in the Floridas had turned to Scots traders to supply essential goods that Madrid did not send—goods essential to pacifying the southern Indian tribes. Through trade the Spanish-Indian coalition against the Americans held fast. With Spain, the Cherokees, Choctaws, Creeks, and Chickasaws were formally allied for mutual protection in the Treaty of Nogales, 1793.[33]

Jefferson and George Rogers Clark had once plotted to incite Indian attacks on frontier families as a ruse to declare war on the natives and force them into signing away their lands. Anthony Wallace, author of *Jefferson and the Indians*, describes Jefferson's "public-relations" strategy whereby he sought to downplay Indian massacres while encouraging settlers to conquer the Indians and terminate their claims to the land. According to Wallace, Jefferson was cold and calculating, prepared to "violate the Bill of Rights, shed blood, and give no quarter in order to eliminate those who did not share his version of liberty!"[34]

Not all Americans were anti-Spanish; in the Northeast, commercial interests saw the Mississippi River trade as a threat because it allowed New Orleans to become a competing market for ports like Philadelphia, Boston, and New York. New Englanders sought to establish trade with Spain with the hope of selling goods into Spain's colonies elsewhere in the Western Hemisphere, which would be shipped from northern ports. Caring little for the backwoods farmers who were shut out from the market, Northeasterners felt that Spain's limits on the Mississippi traffic actually strengthened the Union, keeping the Western states from breaking away because they could not trade independently.[35] When Spain and the United States negotiated the Treaty of San Lorenzo in 1795, resulting in lower duties on American shipments down the lower Mississippi, it delighted the residents of the backwoods and deflated schemes for separating the West from the Union. Some say there were two forces responsible for holding the fledgling Union of disparate states together at this crucial point: the Treaty of San Lorenzo and George Washington.[36]

IN 1800 Jefferson won the presidential election after thirty-six ballots and a successful effort to sway a single elector to switch sides. It had been a close and bitter fight to the end, and neither Federalists nor Republicans would recover quickly. Taking office in early 1801, Jefferson wrote to Meriwether Lewis asking if he would be his private secretary. Lewis was a captain in the army and had been paymaster of the First Infantry, traveling widely to Western forts, performing clerical and personnel tasks. Jefferson sent the letter to General Wilkinson, who was Lewis's commanding officer. The salary would be comparable to what Lewis was already receiving, and he would remain on active duty. "But it would be an easier office, would make you known and be known, to characters of influence in the affairs of our Country, and would give you the advantage of their wisdom. You would, of course, save also the expense of subsistence and lodgings, as you would be one of my family," Jefferson reasoned.[37]

Historians believe that Jefferson chose Lewis for the position because he planned to send the experienced explorer into the West, but Donald Jackson points out that Jefferson did not seek an overland expedition after the Michaux disaster. "During the three years he served as Secretary of State, and four as Vice President, he had done exactly nothing to press for a government expedition. His purchases of geographical books were minimal."[38] Jackson argues that Jefferson hired Lewis as his personal secretary because Lewis knew the Ohio country ("the western country") and the military. He had valuable political information that Jefferson needed.

MERIWETHER Lewis was born in 1774 in Albemarle County, Virginia, at the foot of the Blue Ridge Mountains. Albemarle was

Jefferson's county too, and the Jefferson plantation was not far from the Lewis holdings at Locust Hill. One biographer notes that it was "close enough to Monticello for Jefferson to signal to his young friend Meriwether Lewis, when he wanted him, with a mirror reflecting the sun's rays."[39] The families had been linked in a land company years before, when both Lewis's and Jefferson's fathers, along with other family members, had joined in speculative land ventures. Lewis's father had served with the county Minute Men during the Revolution, becoming a regular army officer. Lieutenant Lewis was still on active duty in 1779 when he died of pneumonia. Meriwether was only five years old at the time; he never overcame his animosity toward the British, whom he held responsible for his father's death.[40]

Meriwether Lewis grew up in a hunter's paradise; by the age of eight he hunted alone at night with his dog. When his mother remarried, the family moved to a new settlement in Georgia. As the eldest son, Meriwether inherited his father's thousand acres at Locust Hill, which relatives managed until he grew older. Georgia was more of a wild frontier than Virginia, and Lewis settled in with the family at the edge of the forest. At fourteen he returned to Albemarle County to take charge of his estate, working with his uncles, Nicholas and William Meriwether.[41] His mother was widowed again in 1791, and Lewis went to Georgia in a carriage to bring her and the younger children home. He took over as master of the estate, turned his efforts to farming corn and wheat, and acquired another thousand acres. He was a young but effective farm manager, paying attention to plants, insects, and weather. Later, in his trek across the West, his ability and interest in the natural world was handy, a result of being well grounded in early hands-on experiences.

In 1796 Meriwether obtained land grants for his siblings and an additional 2,600 acres (worth 26 cents per acre at the time) for himself. His success guaranteed that he would never be destitute.[42] He joined the army and served in a rifle company commanded by William Clark. Clark's military career was cut short when he had to resign and return home to run the family farm, but Lewis continued on, successfully gaining experience and promotions.

Far different from the other young men Jefferson was attracted to, Lewis was not a romantic, an iconoclast, or a mercenary. He was a devoted son to his mother and always cared for his siblings. Although not socially polished, he was sufficiently astute to tailor his behavior to suit whatever situation he found himself in. He may have been attracted to the military not as an escape from home, an avenue for personal gain, or a path to adventure but rather as a way to emulate the heroic father he barely knew. He was financially secure, had strong moral sensibility, and was loyal to his country. Lewis would prove invaluable to Jefferson. Without him, Jefferson's first term would have been a disaster. Lewis even read Jefferson's first State of the Union address before Congress because Jefferson was so anxious about speaking publicly.

Historians do not agree about why or even when Jefferson decided to send Lewis up the Missouri River to explore the Western regions. It may even have been Lewis's idea, though there is no record of Lewis having prompted Jefferson to do so. Just as Jefferson claimed to have originated the John Ledyard trip—which was clearly Ledyard's idea—so too might he have taken advice from Lewis, who worked closely on government affairs with Jefferson from 1801 on. Lewis may indeed have done most of the pretrip planning; with his experience as an army payroll officer and farm owner, he knew how to make plans and arrange supplies. Jefferson's idea of pretrip advice, as seen in his experience with John Ledyard, consisted of the odd idea of tattooing marks on his arm to gauge longitude. Certainly he was not the one who carefully itemized, ordered, and planned the Corps of Discovery's Western expedition.

In any event, together the two men were able to put together what had previously been impossible. With Jefferson's platform as president, Lewis was able to obtain special information, supplies, and materials that others before him had lacked. While Jefferson may have envisioned a lone man like Ledyard or Nolan striking out into the wild, Lewis was trained to work with a team. His military training, something Jefferson lacked, gave him an entirely different perspective on the expedition. It would be made by a group—small, so as not to anger Indians (a bit of advice from George Rogers Clark), yet large enough that it made up a functional unit.

Lewis was not Ledyard, Michaux, or Nolan. He was no romantic, had not attended college, and was trained by the military. As Donald Jackson reminds us, "If there is an antidote to the infectious habit of considering the Lewis and Clark expedition a kind of high-risk romp, a bunch of guys out camping and collecting, it is the realization that Lewis and Clark were army men going by the book."[43] Indeed, Lewis and most of the expedition's participants were men who knew the army, but not from the vantage point of a Wilkinson or a Washington. Their experience was as privates earning five dollars a month. Soldiers, they knew the need for military discipline, and their attitude toward one another and the leadership kept them focused on their task with little interpersonal pettiness, jealousy, or disagreement.

AS PLANS for Meriwether Lewis's secret trip west solidified, Jefferson planned to ask Congress for approval and financing for the expedition in his annual message to Congress scheduled for December 1802, but Secretary of the Treasury Albert Gallatin dissuaded him after seeing a draft of Jefferson's proposed speech. Gallatin thought the expedition should be confidential, because it would move beyond American borders and could be seen as illegal as well as creating potential diplomatic headaches.[44] So on January 18, 1803, Jefferson sent a secret message to Congress asking for approval and financing for an exploratory expedition into Louisiana. He emphasized that the goal would be to establish trade with the Indians while gaining more knowledge of the area and peoples. British fur traders had been encroaching southward from the Great Lakes, developing ties and trading with the Indians, just as the Spanish had long done in southern Louisiana. It would be good to know what tribes were out there and to whom they were loyal. The trip would serve both business and national security. After hearing the proposal, Congress met behind closed doors and agreed to approve an expedition.[45] Several historians now agree that Jefferson camouflaged his real intent, which was to acquire Indian lands. That intent was the real reason it was kept secret: "the red men were believed to be hostile to further cession of their lands," explains Meriwether Lewis's biographer, Richard Dillon.[46]

Indian lands, whether to the west or the south, were vital to Jefferson's vision of how the nation would survive. He had received popular political support because he promised an end to the despised whiskey tax, which hurt farmers in the hinterlands who had no other way to market grain crops except as distilled spirits. When he abolished the tax, Jefferson also got rid of all tax collectors and government inspectors, a very popular measure. How was he to fund government, then? By the sale of public lands to private interests, and by levying tariffs. Selling off land seemed inconsequential; Jefferson believed there was sufficient land for Americans to continue expansion nearly forever. Those lands were still in the hands of Spain, which was weak and fading fast. Indians were certainly also problematic to his vision, but Jefferson planned to move all the Indians, once they had ceded their lands, to a vast Indian country beyond the Mississippi River.

First, however, the government needed to know exactly how many Indians were involved. A reconnaissance by someone as discreet and astute as Meriwether Lewis was essential. While other countries were spending lavishly on scientific explorations around the globe, a paltry $2,500, plus arms and some land grants to the participants on their return, would cover Jefferson's endeavor. To emphasize the value such an expedition would return, he needed to interest Federalists and others who were not so supportive of his agrarian plans. Jefferson told Congress, "The interest of commerce place this principal object within the constitutional powers and cares of Congress, and that it should incidentally advance the geographical knowledge of our own Continent cannot but be an additional gratification." He went on to point out that Spain's interest did not matter. "The nation claiming the territory, regarding this as a literary pursuit which it is in the habit of permitting within its dominions, would not be disposed to view it with jealousy, even if the expiring state of its interests there did not render it a matter of indifference."[47] Congress agreed with Jefferson. He had emphasized the two points they could endorse: commerce and thumbing their nose at Spain.

Once the plan was approved, Lewis and Jefferson worked to make it a reality. Lewis worked tirelessly, obtaining supplies and

sages to each other. If they ever did use the code to communicate, no examples have been found. Jefferson, Wilkinson, and many other figures of the day commonly used codes and ciphers to pass messages; it was an era when mail was entrusted to nearly anyone and might be opened and read at will.

Jefferson made available to Lewis the most recent maps of the West: British maps by Arrowsmith, Mackenzie, Mitchell, and Thornton; French maps by d'Anville and Delisle; and Vancouver's maps of the Pacific Northwest coast. He also had purchased several ships' logs from trips to the Pacific Northwest, which possibly he shared with Lewis as well. Albert Gallatin provided a blank map drawn by the mapmaker Nicholas King, showing all known features; Lewis would add to it as he went, in a sort of fill-in-the-blanks manner. A copy of that 1803 map resides at the Library of Congress.[54]

By March 1803 Lewis had obtained a French passport; within three weeks he also had one from Britain, largely because he already had the French passport in hand.[55] Britain felt no threat from Lewis because Alexander Mackenzie had already thoroughly explored the region in which the crown was interested. The French agreed to grant the passport after meeting with Jefferson. The minister to France wrote to the diplomat Talleyrand in Paris, "The travelers must return by sea. They will find an opportunity on the Northwest coast, even by American ships. That is perhaps the only detail of the expedition in which a French passport might be of some use."[56] Cagily, Jefferson told the British minister it would be only a geographic venture—with no interest in Indian trade. He added that it looked like France was about to "set on foot enterprises of a similar nature," which clinched British backing for the Americans to proceed.[57] Jefferson, who had obtained the passports for Lewis, wrote to him,

"The country of Louisiana having been ceded by Spain to France, and possession by this time probably given, the passport you have from the Minister of France, the representative of the present sovereign of the country, will be a protection with all its subjects and that of the Minister of England will entitle you to the friendly aid of traders of that allegiance with whom you may happen to meet."[58]

All should have been well for Lewis, except that he did not have permission from Spain. In December 1802 the Spanish minister to the United States, Don Carlos Martinez de Yrujo, wrote the minister of foreign affairs in Madrid, Pedro Cevallos, about Lewis's pending trip. Not only did Spain have secret operatives nearly everywhere in the United States, they reported promptly. Madrid knew of the expedition before the American public did. Martinez de Yrujo told Cevallos that Jefferson had asked about sending travelers to explore the Missouri River, going as far as the Pacific, and that he had refused permission. Martinez de Yrujo explained, "The President has been all his life a man of letters, very speculative and a lover of glory, and it would be possible he might attempt to perpetuate the fame of his administration not only by the measures of frugality and economy which characterize him, but also by discovering or attempting at least to discover the way by which the Americans may some day extend their population and their influence up to the coasts of the South Sea [Pacific Ocean]."[59]

When Jefferson approached Martinez de Yrujo about Spain's response to the pending trip, de Yrujo replied that it could not fail to upset his government.[60] Jefferson argued that Lewis's trip would simply determine the existence of a Northwest Passage, but Martinez de Yrujo scoffed. Cook, Vancouver, Mourelle, Bodega, Mackenzie, and Malaspina had disproved the idea of any such passage. Jefferson's entreaty did not alter the Spanish position.[61] One reason for Spain's strong opposition to the expedition was Jefferson's link to Philip Nolan's well-armed incursion on Spanish soil in 1801, just two years earlier.[62]

Jefferson's subterfuge nonetheless continued, as he reported to Congress that Spain did not care about such a "literary and scientific" foray, that their interests in the Western lands were "expiring," and that the American expedition was a "matter of indifference." He also lied to Meriwether Lewis. When Lewis inquired if Spanish officials had approved the venture, Jefferson assured him everything had been arranged—Spain "would not oppose it by force."[63] Certainly small degrees of truth-shading can soften diplomacy and get things accomplished, but in this case Jefferson deliberately deceived someone who would be placed in a dangerous position by the lie. And that person, Lewis, implicitly trusted Jefferson. Of the many lies Jefferson perpetuated throughout his lifetime, telling Meriwether Lewis that the Spanish were agreeable to the venture is one of the most difficult to accept.

Lewis, full of idealism and eager for honor (rather than glory, a very different thing), now gathered up loose ends and prepared to depart. He wrote to his mother at Locust Hill, "The charge of this Expedition is as honorable to myself as it is important to my Country. For its fatigues I find myself perfectly prepared nor do I doubt my health and strength of constitution to bear me through it. I go with the most perfect pre-conviction in my own mind of returning safe and hope, therefore, that you will not suffer yourself to indulge any anxiety for my safety."[64]

Meanwhile, international events were casting the expedition in a new light. Political leaders were pressing Jefferson to move in and take West Florida, noting that the time was right and the risk small. Federalists were upset by Jefferson's slowness, as he relied on diplomacy and merely seemed to buy time. They wanted a war, which would gain them the political support of the Republicans. Alexander Hamilton urged an outright seizure of New Orleans and the Floridas. Hamilton felt that General Wilkinson, now commander of the army in the West, could be key. He was a "man of more than ordinary talent, courage, and enterprise," and Hamilton wanted to use him to take Louisiana from the French.[65] Senate resolutions to support a militia of fifty thousand to seize New Orleans, and allow eighty thousand militia to be called up if needed, were narrowly defeated in February 1801. Federalists and Republicans alike wanted the war with France— only Jefferson hesitated.[66] He had always believed that war with the weakening Spain was imminent; to him, Spain, still in control of Western lands, was the power to worry about.

The nation was excited about the prospect of war in the Southern region, where French and Spanish installations seemed inadequate and easily defeatable. In August 1803 Andrew Jackson ordered his Kentucky militia to be ready to march on a moment's notice. Jefferson ordered a thousand regular army troops and six thousand militia volunteers from Kentucky, Tennessee, and Ohio to move south.[67] As president, Jefferson knew he would need a good reason to justify seizing another nation's land. At a time when European powers were on the verge of igniting another war, the United States might find itself without friends and allies if it committed such a flagrant act.[68]

In Europe, Napoleon Bonaparte was facing difficult odds. He had sent troops to maintain control of French Haiti, but the action had been a failure. Thousands died from disease or by fighting the slave insurrection led by Toussaint-Louverture. The colony siphoned off men and money while France faced defeat

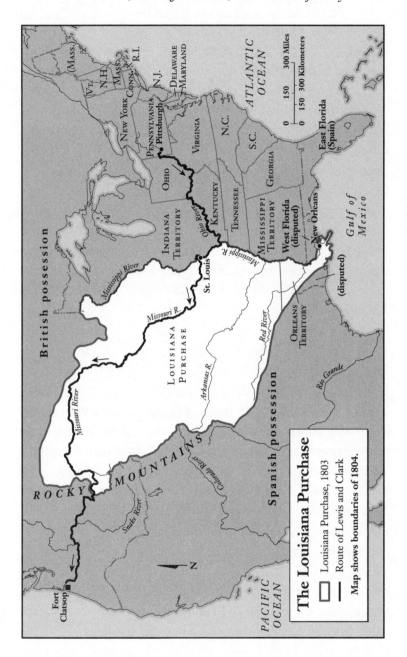

The Louisiana Purchase

☐ Louisiana Purchase, 1803
— Route of Lewis and Clark
Map shows boundaries of 1804.

on European battlefields. Now at war with Britain, France needed the United States as an ally in North America. When American diplomats arrived in Paris in 1803 inquiring if France might be willing to sell the port of New Orleans and West Florida to the United States, Napoleon seized the opportunity. For $15 million he sold all of Louisiana. It seemed a mistake but rather was a diplomatic coup developed by the U.S. minister, Robert Livingston, who was deaf and did not even speak French. On April 30, 1803, the deal was done: Louisiana belonged to the United States. It was not exactly what the budding nation wanted, however. West Florida, with its mild climate and fertile soil, was not included in the deal but reverted to Spain. The Mississippi River could now be freely plied with American flatboats, and America could now deal with the vast expanse beyond the Mississippi. But how?

Spain at once declared the purchase invalid. In December 1795 Spain had offered Louisiana to France in exchange for Haiti. Four years later Napoleon had acquired the territory in exchange for a throne in Italy for Spanish Queen Maria Luisa's brother (which was never given). The negotiations were secret, and Spain included wording to prevent France from passing Louisiana to another country. Napoleon did not keep that promise, instead selling it to the United States.[69]

Louisiana's borders had never been formally delineated. Now the United States claimed that West Florida and all of Texas too were part of Louisiana. Spanish officials, never a party to the negotiations, bristled and fired missives back and forth. Meanwhile Jefferson sent troops to the edge of West Florida, daring the Spanish to react. The president was ready for war with Spain, even eager for it, but Gallatin reminded him that it was not justifiable "even in America" to attack a peaceful country.

While many French citizens were irate because of the loss of Louisiana and clamored to get it back, Americans were not entirely thrilled with the acquisition either. Some Federalists who had earlier clamored for war now viewed the Louisiana Purchase with skepticism. A Boston newspaper described Louisiana as "a great waste, a wilderness unpeopled with any beings except wolves and wandering Indians. . . . We are to give money of which we have too little for land of which we already have too much."[70] In 1803, $15 million was an enormous amount of money. Besides, no one had ever wanted Louisiana—it was New Orleans, and possibly Florida, that had been sought. Acquiring more land only helped agrarian political interests anyway, something that would ensure Jefferson's reelection (indeed, he won in 1804 by a landslide) but hampered the commercial interests of the Eastern states. But only nine senators were Federalists; the nation was rapidly turning Republican, so there was no significant opposition to the ratification of the purchase. On October 20, after two days' discussion, the Senate approved the Louisiana Purchase by a vote of 24 to 7.[71]

Ironically, when ceremonies of transfer were held that autumn in New Orleans, Gen. James Wilkinson officially accepted for the U.S. government. His work as a secret agent for Spain was yet undiscovered, and after the ceremony he sent a report to Spanish officials telling them how the transfer would affect them, advising steps they should take to prevent American incursions into their holdings—and requesting back payments due him for information. Another ceremony was held the following March in St. Louis, and one of the witnesses was Capt. Meriwether Lewis, attending in full-dress uniform. By that time his expedition was no longer a secret.[72]

5

Preparations

It is painful to acknowledge it and to experience it, but it will be much more painful not to use all our forces, while there is still time to remedy it, even though it be at the cost of continual vigilance and no small expense.—The Marquis de Casa Calvo to Pedro Cevallos, regarding U.S. preparations to send an expedition to the Pacific coast[1]

SPANISH OFFICIALS made it clear that Spain intended to retain a large portion of what Jefferson considered to have been included in the Louisiana Purchase. With no official border between French and Spanish territory, it was unclear what France had actually sold to the United States. Historians suggest that France may have been deliberately evasive about the borders, hoping the United States and Spain would clash, allowing France to align itself with whichever side would be more advantageous. Indeed, if Napoleon had been intent merely on obtaining cash for Louisiana, he could have sold it for much more to Spain, whose coffers were far deeper than the fledgling United States.

Louisiana was worth a great deal to Spain as a buffer to keep other powers out of its rich mines, and it would have cooperated with France to regain the territory. But Napoleon may have realized that the inevitable westward expansion of the United States could not be delayed forever, considering Spain's obviously diminishing power in the New World. Nevertheless Louisiana's boundaries would not be determined until 1819. Meanwhile the Spanish court considered that their provinces of Texas and New Mexico extended north to the confluence of the Missouri with the Mississippi River, near St. Louis. And there were hints that Spain would begin constructing forts along these borders.[2]

Relations between Spain and the United States had been turbulent since the outset of Jefferson's presidency. The Mobile Act of 1803 allowed the United States to send troops into lower Louisiana, ostensibly to protect white residents from possible slave uprisings. From there the troops could be moved quickly into West Florida as needed.[3] The act, largely diplomatic blustering, was a futile attempt to coerce Spain into negotiating away the Florida holdings.

"In seeking to extend their empire in the east, the Jeffersonians worked out a simple plan, similar in approach to their old Louisiana strategy," the historian Alexander DeConde explains. "They would claim West Florida as part of Louisiana and threaten to seize it as a legitimate exercise of property rights. Then they would sell West and East Florida. They thus would merge their claim to territory as far east as the Perdido [River] with an offer to buy both Floridas."[4] In the summer of 1803 Jefferson's secretary of state, James Madison, sent James Monroe to Madrid to offer $2.5 million for the Floridas. Still furious about Louisiana's sale, Spain refused. Spain continued to remind the

United States that it had no legal claim to Louisiana in the first place—Spain's treaty with France had specifically forbidden such a deal.

SENDING Lewis and Clark across contested ground was a deliberate, obvious attempt to provoke Spain—it can hardly be considered anything else. Lewis, ready to depart from Philadelphia in early June 1803, sent Jefferson some sketches of the Northwest coast made by the British captain Vancouver, to help in creating a map. Then he sat down and wrote a lengthy letter to William Clark, describing what they were about to embark on. While the letter is long, it succinctly reveals what Lewis believed to be ahead of them.

Washington June 19th 1803

Dear Clark,

. . . From the long and uninterrupted friendship and confidence which has subsisted between us I feel no hesitation in making to you the following communication under the fullest impression that it will be held by you inviolably secret until I see you, or you shall hear again from me.

During the last session of Congress a law was passed in conformity to a private message of the President of the United States, inti[t]led "An Act making an appropriation for extending the external commerce of the United States." The object of this Act as understood by it's framers was to give the sanction of the government to exploring the interior of the continent of North America, or that part of it bordering on the Missouri & Columbia Rivers. This enterprise has been confided to me by the President, and in consequence since the beginning of March I have been engaged in making the necessary preparations for the tour. These arrangements being now nearly completed, I shall set out for Pittsburgh (the intended point of embarcation) about the last of this month, and as soon after as from the state of the water you can reasonably expect me I shall be with you, say about the 10th of August. To aid me in this enterprise I have the most ample and hearty support that the government can give in every possible shape. I am armed with the authority of the Government of the U. States for my protection, so far as its authority or influence extends; in addition to which, the further aid has been given me of liberal passports from the Ministers both of France and England: I am instructed to select from any corps in the army a number of noncommissioned officers and privates not exceeding 12, who may be disposed voluntarily to enter into this service; and am also authorized to engage any other men not soldiers that I may think useful in promoting the objects or success of this expedition. I am likewise furnished with letters of credit, and authorized to draw on the government for any sum necessary for the comfort of myself or party. To all the persons engaged in this service I am authorized to offer the following rewards by way of inducement—1st the bounty (if not a soldier) but in both cases six months pay in advance: 2dly to discharge them from the service if they wish it, immediately on their return from the expedition giving them their arrears of pay clothing &c/ & 3dly to secure to them a portion of land equal to that given by the United States to the officers and soldiers who served in the revolutionary army. This is a sho[r]t view of means with which I am intrusted to carry this plan of the Government into effect. I will now give you a short sketch of my plan of operation: I shall embark at Pittsburgh with a party of recruits eight or nine in number, intended only to manage the boat and are not calculated on as a permanent part of my detatcment; when descending the Ohio it shall be my duty by enquiry to find out and engage some good hunters, stout, healthy, unmarried men, accustomed to the woods, and capable of bearing bodily fatigue in a pretty considerable degree: should any young men answering this discription be found in your neighborhood I would thank you to give information of them on my arivall at the falls of the Ohio; and if possible learn the probability of their engaging in this service, this may be done perhaps by holding out the idea that the direction of this expedition is up the Mississippi to its source, and thence to the lake of the Woods, stating the probable period of absence at about 18 months; if they would engage themselves in a service of this description there would be but little doubt that they would engage in the real design when it became necessary to make it known to them, which I should take care to do before I finally engaged them. The soldiers that will most probably answer this expedition best will be found in some of the companies stationed at Massac, Kaskaskias & Illinois: pardon this digression from the discription of my plan: it is to descend the Ohio in a keeled boat of about ten tons burthen, from Pittsburgh to it's mouth, thence up the Mississippi to the mouth of the Missourie, and up that river as far as it's navigation is practicable with a boat of this discription, there to prepare canoes of bark or raw-hides, and proceed to it's source, and if practicable pass over to the waters of the Columbia or Origan River and by descending it reach the Western Ocean; the mouth of this river lies about one hundred and forty miles South of Nootka-Sound, at which place there is a considerable European Tradeing establishment, and from which it will be easy to obtain a passage to the United States by way of the East-Indies in some of the trading vessels that visit Nootka Sound annually, provided it should be thought more expedient to do so, than to return by the rout I had pursued in my outward bound journey. The present season being already so far advanced, I do not calculate on getting further than two or three hundred miles up the Missourie before the commencement of the ensuing winter. At this point wherever it may be I shall make myself as comfortable as possible during the winter and resume my journey as early in the spring as the ice will permit: should nothing take place to defeat my progress altogether I feel confident that my passage to the Western Ocean can be effected by the end of the next Summer or the beginning of Autumn. In order to subsist my party with some degree of comfort dureing the ensuing winter, I shall engage some French traders at Illinois to attend me to my wintering ground with a sufficient quantity of flour, pork, &c. to serve them plentifully during the winter, and thus be enabled to set out in the Spring with a healthy and vigorous party—so much for the great outlines of this scheem, permit me now to mention partially the objects which it has in view or those which it is desirable to effect through it's means, and then conclude this lengthy communication. You must know in the first place that very sanguine expectations are at this time formed by our Government that the whole of that immense country wartered by the Mississippi and it's tributary streams, Missourie inclusive, will be the property of the U. States in less than 12 Months from this date; but here let me again impress you with the necessity of keeping this matter a perfect secret—in such a state of things therefore as we have every reason to hope, you will readily concieve the importance to the U. States of an early friendly and intimate acquaintance with the tribes that inhabit that country, that they should be early impressed with a just idea of the rising importance of the U. States and of her friendly dispositions towards them, as also her desire to become useful to them by furnishing them through her citizens with such articles by way of barter as may be desired by them or useful to them— the other objects of this mission are scientific, and of course not less interesting to the U. States than to the world generally, such is the ascertaining by celestial observation the geography of the country through which I shall pass; the names of the nations who inhabit it, the extent and limitts of their several possessions, their relation with other tribes and nations, their languages, traditions, and monuments; their ordinary occupations in fishing, hunting, war, arts, and the implements for their food, clothing, and domestic accommodation; the diseases prevalent among them and the remidies they use; the articles of commerce they may need, or furnish, and to what extent; the soil and face of the country; it's growth and vegetable productions, its animals, the miniral productions of every description; and in short to collect the best possible information relative to whatever the country may afford as a tribute to general science.

My Instruments for celestial observation are an excellent set and my supply of Indian presents is sufficiently ample.

Thus my friend you have so far as leasure will at this time permit me to give it you, a summary view of the plan, the means and the objects of this expedition. If therefore there is anything under those circumstances, in this enterprise, which would induce you to participate with me in its fatiegues, it's dangers and it's honors, believe me there is no man on earth with whom I should feel equal pleasure in sharing them as with yourself; I make this communication to you with the privity of the President, who expresses an anxious wish that you would consent to join me in this enterprise; he has authorized me to say that in the event of your accepting this proposition he will grant you a Captain's commission which of course will intitle you to the pay and emoluments attached to that office and will equally with myself intitle you to such portion of land as was granted to officers of similar rank for their Revolutionary services; the commission with which he proposes to furnish you is not to be considered temporary but permanent if you wish it; your situation if joined with me in this mission will in all respects be precisely such as my own. Pray write to me on this subject as early as possible and direct to me at Pittsburgh. Should you feel disposed not to attatch yourself to this party in an official character, and at the same time feel a disposition to accompany me as a friend any part of the way up the Missouri I should be extremely happy in your company, and will furnish you with every aid for your return from any point you might wish it. With sincere and affectionate regard, Your friend & Humble Sevt.

Meriwether Lewis[5]

Lewis clearly knew much about Nootka and the North Pacific trade, but he anticipated that he would reach the coast much farther north than where the mouth of the Columbia sits. And because he anticipated quite a bit of shipping traffic on the West Coast, he planned to return by sea. Clark, with no other information provided to him, would also have believed that was their plan.

Jefferson's instructions to Lewis, which appear in most American history books, illustrate what Jefferson felt should be part of the expedition's historical record. The letter has been lauded as a superior example of Jefferson's vision and complexity, yet it was read and refined before the "final product" emerged, as we see it here.

June 20, 1803

To Captain Meriwether Lewis esq. Capt. Of the 1st regimt. Of Infantry of the U.S. of A.

Your situation as Secretary of the President of the U.S. has made you acquainted with the objects of my confidential message of Jan. 18, 1803 to the legislature; you have seen the act they passed, which, though expressed in general terms, was meant to sanction those objects, and you are appointed to carry them into execution.

Instruments for ascertaining, by celestial observations, the geography of the country through which you will pass, have been already provided. Light articles for barter and presents among the Indians, arms for your attendants, say for from 10 to 12 men, boats, tents, & other traveling apparatus, with ammunition, medicine, surgical instruments and provisions you will have prepared with such aids as the Secretary at War can yield in his department; & from him also you will receive authority to engage among our troops, by voluntary agreement, the number of attendants above mentioned, over whom you, as their commanding officer, are invested with all the powers the laws give in such a case.

As your movements while within the limits of the U.S. will be better directed by occasional communications, adapted to circumstances as they arise, they will not be noticed here. What follows will respect your proceedings after your departure from the United States.

Your mission has been communicated to the ministers here from France, Spain & Great Britain; and through them to their governments: & such assurances given them as to its objects, as we trust will satisfy them. The country of Louisiana having been ceded by Spain to France, and possession by this time probably given, the passport you have from the minister of France, the representative of the present sovereign of the country, will be a protection with all its subjects; & that from the minister of England will entitle you to the friendly aid of any traders of that allegiance with whom you may happen to meet.

The object of your mission is to explore the Missouri river, & such principal stream of it, as, by its course and communication with the waters of the Pacific Ocean, whether the Columbia, Oregon, Colorado, or any other river may offer the most direct & practicable water communication across this continent for the purposes of commerce.

Beginning at the mouth of the Missouri, you will take careful observations of latitude & longitude, at all remarkable points on the river, & especially at the mouths of rivers, at rapids, at islands, & other places & objects distinguished by such natural marks & characters of a durable kind, as that they may with certainty be recognized hereafter. The courses of the river between these points of observation may be supplied by the compass, the log-line & by time, corrected by the observations themselves. The variations of the compass too, in different places, should be noticed.

The interesting points of the portage between the heads of the Missouri, & of the water offering the best communication with the Pacific ocean, should also be fixed by observation, & the course of that water to the ocean, in the same manner as that of the Missouri.

Your observations are to be taken with great pains & accuracy, to be entered distinctly & intelligibly for others as well as yourself, to comprehend all the elements necessary, with the aid of the usual tables, to fix the latitude and longitude of the places at which they were taken, and are to be rendered to the war-office, for the purpose of having the calculations made concurrently by proper persons within the U.S. Several copies of these as well as of your other notes should be made at leisure times, & put into the care of the most trust-worthy of your attendants, to guard, by multiplying them, against the accidental losses to which they will be exposed. A further guard would be that one of these copies be on the paper of the birch, as less liable to injury from damp than common paper.

The commerce which may be carried on with the people inhabiting the line you will pursue, renders a knowledge of those people important. You will therefore endeavor to make yourself acquainted, as far as a diligent pursuit of your journey shall admit, with the names of the nations & their numbers;

- The extent & limits of their possessions
- Their relations with other tribes of nations

- Their language, traditions, monuments
- Their ordinary occupations in agriculture, fishing, hunting, war, arts, & the implements for these
- Their food, clothing, & domestic accommodations
- The diseases prevalent among them, & the remedies they use
- Moral and physical circumstances which distinguish them from the tribes we know
- Peculiarities in their laws, customs & dispositions
- And articles of commerce they may need or furnish, & to what extent.

And, considering the interest which every nation has in extending & strengthening the authority of reason & justice among the people around them, it will be useful to acquire what knowledge you can of the state of morality, religion, & information among them; as it may better enable those who may endeavor to civilize and instruct them, to adapt their measures to the existing notions & practices of those on whom they are to operate.

Other objects worthy of notice will be:

- The soil & face of the country, its growth & vegetable productions, especially those not of the U.S.
- The animals of the country generally, & especially those not known in the U.S.
- The remains or accounts of any which may be deemed rare or extinct
- The mineral productions of every kind; but more particularly metals, limestone, pit coal, & saltpeter; salines & mineral waters, noting the temperature of the last, & such circumstances as may indicate their character

- Volcanic appearances
- Climate, as characterized by the thermometer, by the proportion of rainy, cloudy, & clear days, by lightning, hail, snow, ice, by the access & recess of frost, by the winds prevailing at different seasons, the dates at which particular plants put forth or lose their flower, or leaf, times of appearance of particular birds, reptiles or insects.

Although your route will be along the channel of the Missouri, yet you will endeavor to inform yourself, by inquiry, of the character & extent of the country watered by its branches & especially on its Southern side. The North River or Rio Bravo which runs into the Gulf of Mexico, and the North River or Rio Colorado which runs into the Gulf of California, are understood to be the principal streams heading opposite to the waters of the Missouri, and running Southwardly. Whether the dividing grounds between the Missouri & them are mountains or flat lands, what are their distance from the Missouri, the character of the intermediate country, & the people inhabiting it, are worthy of particular inquiry. The Northern waters of the Missouri are less to be inquired after, because they have been ascertained to a considerable degree, & are still in a course of ascertainment by English traders, and travelers. But if you can learn any thing certain of the most Northern source of the Mississippi, & of its position relatively to the lake of the woods, it will be interesting to us.

Two copies of your notes at least and as many more as leisure will admit, should be made & confided to the care of the most trusty individuals of your attendants. Some account too of the path of the Canadian traders from the Mississippi, at the mouth of the Wisconsin to where it strikes the Missouri, & of the soil and rivers in its course, is desirable.

In all your intercourse with the natives, treat them in the most friendly & conciliatory manner which their own conduct will admit; allay all jealousies as to the object of your journey, satisfy them of its innocence, make them acquainted with the position, extent, character, peaceable & commercial dispositions of the U.S., of our wish to be neighborly, friendly & useful to them, & of our dispositions to a commercial intercourse with them; confer with them on the points most convenient as mutual emporiums, and the articles of most desirable interchange for them & us. If a few of their influential chiefs, within practical distance, wish to visit us, arrange such a visit with them, and furnish them with authority to call on our officers, on their entering the U.S. to have them conveyed to this place at the public expense. If any of them should wish to have some of their young people brought up with us, & taught such arts as may be useful to them, we will receive, instruct & take care of them. Such a mission, whether of influential chiefs or of young people, would give some security to your own party. Carry with you some matter of the kinepox; inform those of them with whom you may be, of its efficacy as a preservative from the smallpox; & instruct & encourage them in the use of it. This may be especially done wherever you winter.

As it is impossible for us to foresee in what manner you will be received by those people, whether with hospitality or hostility, so is it impossible to prescribe the exact degree of perseverance with which you are to pursue your journey. We value too much the lives of citizens to offer them to probable destruction. Your numbers will be sufficient to secure against the unauthorized opposition of individuals or of small parties; but if a superior force, authorized or not authorized, by a nation, should be arrayed against your further passage, and inflexibly determined to arrest it, you must decline its farther pursuit, and return. In the loss of yourselves, we should lose also the information you will have acquired. By returning safely with that, you may enable us to renew the essay with better calculated means. To your own discretion therefore must be left the degree of danger you may risk, and the point at which you should decline, only saying we wish you to err on the side of your safety, and to bring back your party safe even if it be with less information.

As far up the Missouri as the white settlements extend, an intercourse will probably be found to exist between them & the Spanish posts of St. Louis opposite Cahokia, or St. Genevieve opposite Kaskaskia. From still further up the river, the traders may furnish a conveyance for letters. Beyond that, you may perhaps be able to engage Indians to bring letters for the government to Cahokia or Kaskaskia, on promising that they shall there receive such special compensation as you shall have stipulated with them. Avail yourself of these means to communicate to us, at seasonable intervals, a copy of your journal, notes & observations, of every kind, putting into cipher whatever might do injury if betrayed.

Should you reach the Pacific Ocean, inform yourself of the circumstances which may decide whether the furs of those parts may not be collected as advantageously at the head of the Missouri (convenient as is supposed to the waters of the Colorado & Oregon or Columbia) as at Nootka sound, or any other point of that coast; and that trade be consequently conducted through the Missouri & U.S. more beneficially than by the circumnavigation now practiced.

On your arrival on that coast endeavor to learn if there be any port within your reach frequented by the sea-vessels of any nation, & to send two of your trusty people back by sea, in such way as they shall judge shall appear practicable, with a copy of your notes: and should you be of opinion that the return of your party by the way they went will be eminently dangerous, then ship the whole, & return by sea, by the way either of Cape Horn, or the Cape of Good Hope, as you shall be able. As you will be without money, clothes or provisions, you must endeavor to use the credit of the U.S. to obtain them, for which purpose open letters of credit shall be furnished you, authorizing you to draw upon the Executive of the U.S. or any of its officers, in any part of the world, on which drafts can be disposed of, & to apply with our recommendations to the consuls, agents, merchants, or citizens of any nation with which we have intercourse, assuring them, in our name, that any aids they may furnish you, shall be honorably repaid, and on demand. Our consuls Thomas Hewes at Batavia in Java, William Buchanan in the Isles of France & Bourbon & John Elmslie at the Cape of Good Hope will be able to supply your necessities by drafts on us.

Should you find it safe to return by the way you go, after sending two of your party round by sea, or with your whole party, if no conveyance by sea can be found, do so; making such observations on your return, as may serve to supply, correct or confirm those made on your outward journey.

On re-entering the U.S. and reaching a place of safety, discharge any of your attendants who may desire & deserve it, procuring for them immediate payment of all arrears of pay & clothing which may have incurred since their departure, and assure them that they shall be recommended to the liberality of the legislature for the grant of a soldier's portion of land each, as proposed in my message to Congress: & repair yourself with your papers to the seat of government to which I have only to add my sincere prayer for your safe return.

To provide, on the accident of your death, against anarchy, dispersion & the consequent danger to your party, and total failure of the enterprise, you are hereby authorized, by any instrument signed & written in your own hand, to name the person among them who shall succeed to the command on your decease, and by like instruments to change the nomination from time to time as further experience of the characters accompanying you shall point out superior fitness: and all the powers and authorities given to yourself are, in the event of your death, transferred to, & vested in the successor so named, with further power to him, and his successors in like manner to name each his successor, who, on the death of his predecessor, shall be invested with all the powers & authorities given to yourself.

Given under my hand at the city of Washington this 20th day of June 1803.

TH: J. Pr. U.S. of A.[6]

After looking over a draft of Jefferson's instructions for Lewis, Madison pointed out that the word "commerce" would be effective at staving off potential critics of "the illicit principal objects of the measure."[7] The reason for Lewis's Pacific coast journey was carefully obscured but is similar to that of another venture, which must have influenced Jefferson—the Billings expedition across Siberia. Commissioned by Catherine the Great, John Ledyard had encountered it in his travels. Catherine patterned the instructions for Billings after those Peter the Great had used when he sponsored Vitus Bering's two trips to the Arctic Ocean and to western North America—which in turn were similar to those given to men sent to conquer Siberia in the 1600s.

In 1733 the Russian Senate had instructed Bering in how to deal with native peoples: "You are to treat them kindly and not to resort to violence or act with brutality but to use persuasion to the end that they will send one of their best men with you to Her Imperial Majesty. You are to explain that they will not be harmed or detained, that above all on the journey both here and back to their country they will be conducted with every convenience and will be rewarded by Her Imperial Majesty's mercy." Bering was to record native language, writing down "expressions and names of things."[8] The 1733 voyage was a Senate secret, and references to scientific purposes were used to conceal the true objectives of the North American and Arctic expeditions from foreigners and the public.[9] The scientific objectives covered Bering's failure to gather information about other nations' positions on the coast or to discover mineral wealth as Spain had done. Upon his return, the scientific discoveries of Bering's trip were emphasized in order to silence critics and deflect foreign animosity.

Like Bering, who disguised his voyage as a scientific venture that sought to discover the Northwest Passage, Meriwether Lewis was sent to reconnoiter British, Spanish, and even Russian presence in the Northwest. Like the Russians, Jefferson and

Lewis coordinated a trip that was not really scientific but rather political, and designed to establish a hold on the region. Just as it was for Russia, the Pacific coast lay in the only logical direction for American expansion. Early in the trip Lewis gathered specimens of natural plants, animals, and minerals, and made efforts to send them back to Jefferson in a highly visible manner. Critics today point out that some of his samples—a common magpie and prairie dogs, for instance—were not significant finds. Lewis was going through the motions of sending something, anything back east to support the basis for the public objectives of the trip.

Interestingly, both Bering and Billings had been instructed to send back Indians and gather vocabulary from natives, which the Lewis and Clark party did as well. Bering's work had been published by the time of Lewis & Clark's expedition and was likely a part of Jefferson's pretrip planning. How much Jefferson was influenced by the Russian exploration efforts has not been thoroughly examined, but it is clear that the Russians were active in the Pacific Northwest, tangling directly with Spain and eventually emerging as a trade partner with them. Less than a decade later the Russians established Fort Ross on the coast north of San Francisco Bay to supply their local trade ships.

Jefferson took advice from a few others regarding the trip. Levi Lincoln, the attorney general from 1801 to 1804, reminded Jefferson to expect vituperative attacks from his political enemies regarding the expedition. He suggested that the project's focus expand beyond what was ostensibly a spy mission to include observations about the Indians that related to "the improvement of the mind and the preservation of the body," observing Indians' religious ideas, their morals and values, and view on property ownership. That way, Lincoln explained to Jefferson, even if the project was an abject failure, its public purpose would remain noble. "If the enterprise appears to be an attempt to advance [religion and morality] it will by many people, on that account be justified, however calamitous the issue."[10] He added that Lewis could bring the cowpox vaccine (identified by Edward Jenner in the latter part of the eighteenth century) to vaccinate those Indians who had not contracted smallpox. Lincoln's suggestions were adopted, giving the venture the righteous, humane touch it had lacked.

As Lewis outfitted and prepared, Jefferson peppered him with personal requests: to repay an old friend for a wine shipment, to search out and procure a "leopard skin" for a saddle pad, to have Jefferson's watch repaired. Lewis purchased the personal items Jefferson requested, including a "Virginia blanket" and "fleecy socks," and had Jefferson's watch cleaned. He reported that he tried—though unsuccessfully—to find a leopard-skin saddle pad.[11] Lewis completed his preparations by the end of June, writing a promissory note to Jefferson for $103.93 that he borrowed from the president. He wrote to his mother at Locust Hill, telling her about the upcoming trip and reassuring her that he would be as safe as if he were at home. He directed her to pay for his younger brother's education at William and Mary College from his funds. He included $30 for his sister and her husband, along with congratulations on their new son.[12]

On July 4, 1803, Jefferson wrote to Lewis, telling him that his small party of twelve men would be in danger from Indians and probably should try to return home from the Pacific coast by sea. "You may find it imprudent to hazard a return the same way, and may be forced to seek a passage round by sea, in such vessels as you may find on the Western coast." Without money he would need a letter of credit, which that letter would serve as. After receiving the letter, Lewis departed for Pittsburgh, the official launch site of the expedition.[13] Low water made the trip to St. Louis difficult, so Lewis hired farmers to pull the flatboat down-river with oxen from shore.

Clark joined Lewis at Louisville, Kentucky, and they arrived in St. Louis that fall—too late to set out on a trip upriver. They set up Camp Dubois on the American (eastern) side of the Mississippi River, along the mouth of the Wood River. There they spent the winter packing supplies and training, Lewis traveling to nearby St. Louis to arrange some matters of the trip. By October 1803 Lewis expected that the tightfisted Congress would be upset that he still had not entered the Missouri River. He offered to appease critics for his tardy departure by spending time exploring the area south of the Missouri to Santa Fe during the coming winter. Jefferson quickly vetoed the idea, telling Lewis he was planning to ask Congress for about $12,000 to fund expeditions up the Red River, the Arkansas River, and other rivers that fed into the Missouri and Mississippi. He urged Lewis to stick to finding a direct water route to the Pacific, "and therefore not to be delayed or hazarded by any episodes whatever."[14]

While Lewis was waiting at Camp Dubois that October, chomping at the bit to be off to the West, Jefferson delivered a report to Congress about the new Louisiana: "The precise boundaries of Louisiana, westward of the Mississippi, though very extensive, are at present involved in some obscurity. Data are equally wanting to assign with precision its northern extent. . . ."[15]

By March 1804 Congress was taunting Spain by urging the president to send exploration parties into Louisiana. The House Committee on Commerce and Manufactures reported that the area in question was the region between Spain (on the south) and Great Britain (on the north), extending to the Pacific Ocean. Jefferson and Congress had now pushed Louisiana's boundaries to include not only Texas but Oregon as well.[16]

When officials in New Spain heard of the Louisiana Purchase they assumed that war was inevitable—how could so much hard-fought territory be given up so easily? They began preparing for battle. In Havana, plans for a naval blockade of the Potomac, Delaware, and Mississippi river ports were quickly put in place. Spanish troops in West Florida were placed on alert, and reinforcements were added to the fifteen hundred men stationed on the border at Nacogdoches along the Sabine River.[17]

6

The Perfect Bait

*Even though I realize it is not an easy undertaking, chance
might proportion things in such a way that it might be
successful.—Letter from Nemesio Salcedo, Commander-in-
Chief of the Interior Provinces, to Fernando de Chacón,
Governor of New Mexico, regarding the capture of
Meriwether Lewis and his party, May 1804*[1]

WHILE Meriwether Lewis was shaking hands with Spanish
governor Carlos Dehault Delassus during the transfer of
territories ceremonies held at St. Louis in March 1804, others
were moving to halt Lewis's planned trip into Spanish territory.
The Marquis de Casa Calvo warned that Lewis and Jefferson
planned to have a port on the Pacific coast within five years and
needed to be stopped immediately. Casa Calvo wrote to the commanding general of the Internal Provinces, Brigadier Don
Nemesio Salcedo y Salcedo, stationed in Chihuahua, to order
Lewis's arrest to prevent "the hasty and gigantic steps which our
neighbors are taking towards the South Sea, entering by way of
the Missouri River."[2]

In December 1803 Lewis had met with Delassus and given him copies of his French and British passports, requesting permission to travel up the Missouri River "in order to fulfill his mission of discoveries and observations," according to Delassus. But the Spanish official would not allow him to pass upriver, opposing the idea in the name of the King." Lewis agreed to wait for word to come from Madrid before spring, when the time would be right to head into the Northwest. He reassured Delassus that he and his men would remain camped at a site along the Wood River, on the American side of the Mississippi, until spring. Delassus told Salcedo and Casa Calvo that "he surprised me for not having provided himself with a passport from our Spanish Minister in Philadelphia; that if he had a passport he could have removed all difficulty." Certainly Lewis must have been frustrated by Jefferson's failure to take care of diplomatic permissions as promised. Jefferson did ask permission from De Yrujo, the minister in Philadelphia, who refused the request. The president ignored his refusal and reassured Lewis that everything had been approved.[3]

Delassus liked Lewis, calling him intelligent and recognizing his "reputation of being a very well educated man and of many talents." Lewis got along well with the Spaniard; he liked Delassus for his "abundant politeness," finding him friendly and amenable. Both were military men, responsible to superiors. Both men understood the other's position, yet Lewis wrote that Spanish officials in St. Louis rightly feared Delassus—"he has been pretty tiranical with them," he explained.

Lewis's appealing manner facilitated his efforts to glean useful information during each of his trips from the camp on Wood River to offices and shops in St. Louis. He requested records from officials and tried to gather information about census data, maps, and other information until eventually the Spanish became suspicious, adopting a guarded attitude. He tried to estimate how many Americans were in Louisiana as squatters or emigrants, and how easy it might be to get the whites to abandon their property on the west side of the Mississippi River and relocate east, so that Jefferson could move Indians to the lands west of the Mississippi. Lewis told Jefferson that until Americans controlled Louisiana, "every thing must be obtained by stealth."[4]

The winter dragged on. Clark trained the men at camp and made game-hunting forays while Lewis gathered information from any sources he could find in St. Louis. He collected specimens, such as a horned lizard, and maps of the region, which he sent on to Jefferson, along with ore samples of lead, silver, and salt. He obtained the minerals from fur traders who had acquired them from Indians living within Spanish boundaries.

Lewis and his men waited, determined to accomplish the trip. In March Gen. James Wilkinson, acting as an agent for Spain, wrote a secret missive to Casa Calvo in New Orleans, describing Meriwether Lewis's objectives and urging Spain to stop him. He suggested that couriers pass the word quickly to officials in Chihuahua and Santa Fe "to detach a sufficient body of chasseurs to intercept Captain Lewis and His party who are on the Missouri River, and force them to retire or take them prisoners."[5] Wilkinson's actions certainly appear to be another attempt to protect his own commercial interests and render himself invaluable to someone. But was he betraying his country? Was he trying to protect Spain, from whom he sporadically received chunks of cash? Perhaps his actions were part of a different plan. The historian Warren Cook points out that "the possibility must not be overlooked that, rather than aiding Madrid, he may have been setting the stage for incidents that would provide an excuse to de-clare war and invade Spanish borderlands."[6]

Certainly Jefferson and most Americans had been eager to go to war with Spain, in order to seize lands from a country they knew was only halfheartedly supporting its North American holdings. Spain was mired in political battles in Europe, and most Spanish colonists held little loyalty to Madrid. Yet Jefferson was often reminded that Americans needed a reason to attack a peaceful country or they could never expect backing from other European powers. Lewis, nearly ready to depart, was the perfect bait. Now that knowledge of his exploration was public, any at-tack on the Corps of Discovery by Spanish interests could be viewed as reason enough to unleash troops along the border of West Florida and eastern Texas, troops who could capture terri-tory the country wanted. Perhaps Louisiana had some value after all, if parties roaming through it became martyrs to the cause of U.S. expansion.

Casa Calvo reacted to Wilkinson's warning, writing to Pedro Cevallos in Madrid that he planned to stop U.S. progress toward the Pacific. The upstart nation was moving too hastily to take possession of and explore Louisiana, and Spain continued to dis-agree with France and the United States about the legality of the sale. The Americans were now claiming the headwaters of the Missouri River and began "extending their designs" to the Pacific Ocean, which "forces us necessarily to become active and to has-ten our steps in order to cut off the gigantic steps of our neigh-bors if we wish, as it is our duty, to preserve intact the dominions of the King and to prevent ruin and destruction of the *Provincias Internas* and of the Kingdom of New Spain." Casa Calvo sug-gested that the "only means which presents itself is to arrest Captain Merry Weather and his party, which cannot help but pass through the nations neighboring New Mexico, its presidios or *rancherías*. A decisive and vigorous blow will prevent immense expenditures and even countless disagreeable replies which must originate between the respective governments, and immediately we are impelled to act out of the necessity of the moment."[7]

This was easy for Casa Calvo to say, comfortably ensconced at New Orleans; Lewis was much farther north, and in a different jurisdiction. Perhaps Casa Calvo could see the larger picture. "What other end can the repeated designs and incursions of the Americans have, designs seen even earlier in the unfortunate one, Philip Nolan." Nolan, the horse thief who had corresponded with Jefferson, had created a stir in New Mexico when he and his heavily armed band were routed. Fears that Lewis might be planning a similar incursion could not be ignored. The Corps of Discovery was indeed well armed and had been purchasing vast quantities of supplies. "We must not lose time," Casa Calvo cautioned; immediate action was imperative. He urged that "the most efficacious steps be taken to arrest the referred to Captain Merry and his followers, who, according to notices, number 25 men, and to seize their papers and instruments that may be found on them."[8] The Americans were "making themselves masters of our rich possessions, which they desire." Casa Calvo admitted that "it is painful to acknowledge it and to experience it, but it will be much more painful not to use all our forces, while there is still time to remedy it, even though it be at the cost of continual vigilance and no small expense."[9]

A flurry of letters among Spanish officials followed, alerting Nemesio Salcedo, commanding general of the Interior Provinces, and Joseph de Yturrigaray, viceroy of Mexico. All were alert to the situation, but bureaucratic ennui set in. Although none of them could ignore the festering situation that promised to involve Spain, no one wished to be responsible for starting an incident that might cost him his appointment. Moreover it took time for these missives, which included copies of earlier letters, to travel between Spanish posts. In Chihuahua, Namesio Salcedo tried to expedite delivery time by sending his letter to Casa Calvo in New Orleans via Cuba. It had taken two months for Casa Calvo's previous letter to reach Salcedo. Such slow communication in a government that allowed little independent action by officials, while diplomatic attention was largely focused elsewhere, meant that little could be efficiently accomplished. It would not be until several months later, in January 1805, that Pedro Cevallos wrote to Casa Calvo confirming that the king had received his letters of warning about Lewis, and had ordered the Spanish minister in Philadelphia to lodge an official protest with the U.S. government "against so manifest an offense against the sovereignty of the King."[10] Meanwhile Spanish officials in North America, believing the government would be solidly behind them, had begun taking efforts to stop the Americans. With no assistance expected to arrive from Madrid, they looked to one other resource at hand: Indians.

General Salcedo agreed with Casa Calvo that it was "very prudent and necessary that on our part they be impeded and if it may not be possible," that the Spanish at least follow the American expedition's progress. He suggested that a party be sent out to find Lewis and to gather information from Indians who might have encountered his party. But that would mean providing trade goods for barter with the Indians, and hiring Indian-language translators. In a letter to Joaquín del Réal Alencaster, the governor of New Mexico, Salcedo advised that "Nothing would be more useful than the apprehension of Merry, and even though I

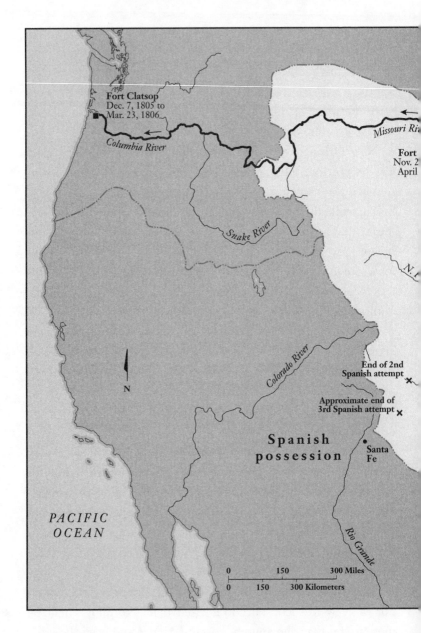

British possession

Route of Lewis and Clark

■ Winter camps
— Route of Lewis and Clark

Map shows boundaries of 1804.

Mississippi River

NEW YORK

PENNSYLVANIA
Pittsburgh
Aug. 31, 1803

End of 1st Spanish attempt to intercept Lewis and Clark

INDIANA TERRITORY

OHIO

✕
End of 4th Spanish attempt

Camp River Dubois
Dec. 12, 1803 to May 14, 1804

Cincinnati

VIRGINIA

Missouri River

St. Louis

Ohio River

Louisville

KENTUCKY

LOUISIANA PURCHASE

Mississippi River

NORTH CAROLINA

Arkansas River

TENNESSEE

SOUTH CAROLINA

MISSISSIPPI TERRITORY

GEORGIA

ORLEANS TERRITORY

West Florida (disputed)

East Florida (Spain)

(disputed)

realize it is not an easy undertaking, chance might proportion things in such a way that it might be successful, for which reason it will not be superfluous for Your Excellency to give notice of this matter to the Indians, interesting their friendship and notions of generosity, telling them that they will be well compensated."[11]

Believing that Lewis represented a danger, Salcedo wrote to Cevallos in Madrid on May 8, 1804, that Casa Calvo's warning would be heeded. Salcedo had "sent a party of Comanche Indians or others of those who are affected to us to reconnoiter the country as far as the banks of the Missouri river in order to examine if the expedition of Merry has penetrated into those territories, to acquire all possible knowledge of its progress, and even to stop them, making efforts to apprehend it."[12]

In April, hectic last-minute preparations had kept Lewis and Clark busy. The St. Louis merchants and fur traders Manuel Lisa and François Marie Benoit were making it difficult for Lewis to get the expedition under way. "Damn Manuel and triply damn Mr. B.," Lewis wrote. "They give me more vexation and trouble than their lives are worth. I have dealt very plainly with these gentlemen. In short, I have come to an open rupture with them. I think them both scoundrels and they have given me abundant proofs of their unfriendly disposition towards our Government and its measures."[13]

When finally under way on May 14, 1804, the Corps of Discovery numbered nearly fifty men. Poling upriver against the current, they met traders coming downriver with furs. Lewis encountered a French fur trader who told him that letters sent to the Osages by Auguste Chouteau telling them about the transfer of Louisiana to the United States had been received by the Indians. They refused to believe it and burned the letters.[14] The trader may have wanted to intimidate Lewis and Clark, who surely began to wonder what they would encounter ahead.

Once Lewis and Clark left the Wood River campsite to head north, the Spaniards began playing a game of catch-up. Although they were unprepared and unable to stop the Corps's progress, they stayed well aware of its movements from St. Louis. Governor Delassus in St. Louis reported that the Americans were "already calculating the profit which they will obtain from the mines."[15] A New Orleans newspaper carried stories about the trip's progress, and even the king in Madrid knew of the situation.[16]

At the same time Spain was encountering problems on the border of West Florida, where Jefferson had sent U.S. troops in an effort to dislodge the southern Indians. American residents in West Florida far outnumbered the Hispanic residents and French colonists, and the presence of troops only added to the threat of an uprising. Cherokees and Chickasaws owned most of Tennessee; most of Georgia was held by Creeks and Cherokees. Chocktaws, Chickasaws, and Creeks held Mississippi and Alabama. Florida was home to displaced Creeks, known as Seminoles, on Spanish land. All were strong tribes, and none were allied to the United States. Jefferson intended to obtain their land as well as Spain's. Eventually, however, he would acquire 200,000 square miles of Indian lands in 9 of today's states, through 32 treaties made with a dozen tribes.[17]

Warren Cook was the first to recognize from the archival records Spain's active efforts to halt the Lewis and Clark expedition. Using archival records from Madrid, Seville, Mexico City, and Santa Fe, Cook reconstructed the attempts to capture Lewis and the Corps of Discovery. He notes that "the fact that orders to check Meriwether Lewis actually got beyond the planning stage and that *four successive expeditions* set out from Santa Fe for this purpose between 1804 and 1806 has virtually eluded historians. . . . The Spanish made repeated efforts of considerable magnitude to intercept Lewis and Clark, and came surprisingly and dangerously close to achieving their objective."[18]

Apache couriers arrived in Santa Fe on May 14, 1804—the day Lewis and Clark pushed off upriver—with letters that laid out Spanish plans to apprehend the Americans. Plans included relying on Indian scouts and mounting an expedition that would feign a search for Coronado's elusive lost Mountain of Gold. That ploy, so innocuous in light of centuries of just such Spanish expeditions across the continent, would prevent Lewis and any U.S. Indian allies from growing suspicious of Spanish parties moving through the area.[19]

Heeding warnings from Salcedo and Casa Calvo, Governor Chacón readied an expedition to pursue Lewis. Pedro Vial, an experienced French explorer and guide, was enlisted to lead the effort. Vial knew the region well: he had pioneered the Santa Fe Trail and had years of experiences with the Indians. He would be assisted by José Jarvet, a Philadelphia-born Presbyterian who had spent years living with the Pawnees while pretending to be French. Vial and Jarvet led thirty mounted soldiers out of Santa Fe on August 1, 1804. At Taos, ten militiamen and ten Indians joined the group. By September 3 the fifty-two men reached the Platte River. Two days later they stopped at a Pawnee village in what is now central Nebraska.[20]

The Pawnees welcomed Vial's party enthusiastically. Twenty French traders were staying in the village, and they described Lewis and Clark's activities. Vial wrote in his trip diary that the Americans were attempting to "take over the government" of the area by giving gifts to the Indians. "In every village they pass, large gifts are made to all chiefs and principal men and said chiefs are induced to surrender medals and patents in their possession, given by the Spanish government." He warned the chiefs not to cooperate, "telling them they do not know the Americans but in the future they will."[21]

While Vial discussed the situation with the Pawnees on the Platte, Lewis and Clark were on the Missouri River near the mouth of the Niobrara, along the Nebraska–South Dakota border, about seventy miles from present-day Yankton.

On August 1, the day Vial's party departed Santa Fe, Lewis and Clark had been at the mouth of the Platte River, waiting for their first meeting with Indians. In his diary William Clark explained that they would "send for Some of the Chiefs . . . to let them know of the Change of Government, the wishes of our government to Cultivate friendship with them, the objects of our journey and to present them with Some Small presents." It was the first time the Lewis and Clark expedition had counciled with Indians, and the first they had met in six hundred miles of travel. During the night their two horses either ran off or were stolen. A deserter, a Frenchman named La Liberté, ran off too. The situation was tense. Clark noted in his diary: "Every man on his guard and ready for anything."[22] Would the Plains tribes allow them to pass? The next day a group of Otoe and Missouri Indians, accompanied by a Frenchman, arrived and swapped watermelons for roasted meat and flour.

When Moses Reed, one of the expedition recruits, also deserted, Clark sent a party after him with orders to "put him to Death" if he resisted.[23] A few days later he was brought back to camp, tried, and punished by running the gantlet four times as members of the expedition struck him.

The Corps moved upriver to winter with the Mandans near

the center of present-day North Dakota. They built log quarters
and remained at Fort Mandan until April 7, 1805, when the keel-
boat went back downriver to St. Louis carrying items of interest
for Jefferson, a few passengers, and an Arikara chief who had
agreed to visit the president. That same day the rest of the expedition headed upriver. It now numbered thirty-three, including a
French Canadian interpreter named Charbonneau, his young Indian wife, Sacagawea, and their two-month-old baby, Jean Baptiste. Sacagawea would be their only "dependence for a friendly
negociation with the Snake Indians on whom we depend for
horses to assist us in our portage from the Missouri to the Columbia river," Lewis wrote.

Meanwhile, Vial took several Pawnee leaders back to Santa
Fe for gifts. Salcedo sent Vial's diary on to Madrid, warning that
the Americans were intent on establishing a port on the Pacific
coast for Asian trade. He asked what to do next.

Other concerns crowded Lewis and Clark from Spanish attention, but the Americans remained a threat, stimulating
Madrid to build up its military strength in the province of Texas
to its highest level—1,273 armed soldiers as well as Pawnees and
Kiowas who were allied with Spain. If Spain could not prevent
France from selling Louisiana to the Americans, at least she
could try to restrict U.S. boundaries to the narrowest possible region.[24] Meanwhile Meriwether Lewis and his expedition were
largely ignored by Americans as the Florida boundary issue grew
in urgency.

Jefferson made it clear to Spanish officials in America that
Spain should not interfere with the Louisiana Purchase. Americans would not only fight for Louisiana, they would attack the
Floridas as well. Always eager for a fight with Spain, Jefferson
seemed to be continually tossing challenges at them. Perhaps he

thought his connections with France would serve him well. But when Monroe arrived in France on his way to Madrid in October 1804, he was surprised to learn that France would not support the United States in extending the borders of Louisiana to include West Florida; French officials chastised America for trying to push expansion beyond the accepted boundaries. Napoleon Bonaparte also criticized the United States for using dealings with France as a springboard to justify aggression against Spain—which was clearly what Jefferson had been doing. In December 1804 Spain declared war on Britain, which brought France to the side of its neighbor and sister Catholic country. With that, Jefferson had no hope of gaining support from France for any actions he yearned to take against Spanish holdings in America. Incursions would bring diplomatic problems if not full-scale war, and the United States would have to rely on Britain, Jefferson's archrival.[25]

In the spring of 1805, Spanish troops moved to the Texas frontier; U.S. militia units moved to Natchitoches, the closest U.S. post to Texas. Residents sensed imminent war and were eager for combat: minor fights erupted spontaneously and were soundly defeated by Spanish forces. Shiploads of reinforcements from Havana and Mexico arrived in West Florida and Texas. Spanish warships laid to in Havana harbor, ready to blockade American ports. Troops moved in all along the Texas border, expecting Americans to mount a hostile assault.

Farther north, the Spanish made a second attempt to catch Lewis in the fall of 1805, when Governor Alencaster, who had replaced Chacón, sent co-commanders Vial and Jarvet out again, this time with two *carabineros* (frontier guards) and fifty militia troopers. Four French trappers and traders accompanied them as scouts and interpreters. They went through Taos, moving only at

night to avoid incurring an Indian attack. They planned to go to
the Pawnee village at the head of the Kansas River. There they
would split up, sending militiamen back with information about
Lewis's progress, while the French traders would head downstream to St. Louis by canoe, spying as they went. Vial and Jarvet
would winter with the Pawnees, securing their loyalty to Spain.
"The Spanish plans were well laid," according to Meriwether
Lewis's biographer, Richard Dillon.[26]

Vial left on November 5, 1805, passing herds of buffalo before his entourage reached the Arkansas River. Near the junction
of the Purgatoire and Arkansas rivers in present-day Colorado,
Indians they did not recognize began following them, and during
the night about a hundred of them attacked the Spanish camp in
three waves. They finally left after a three-hour battle, but attacked again when the party began moving out the next morning,
looting supplies and ammunition. Vial was forced to abandon his
effort and return to Santa Fe. "There he urged that a fort be constructed on the Arkansas to protect New Mexico's flank from
Lewis, and begged that larger forces, with more munitions, be
sent out to prevent such a disaster as had overtaken him," Dillon
writes.[27]

During most of 1805, troops or militia were moved around
North America like pawns on a chessboard—yet neither Spain
nor the United States dared to make the first move. On December 3 Jefferson delivered a most inflammatory address to Congress, urging war on Spain. In spite of months of discussion and
debate in Congress, many doubted the West was worth a fight.
War with Spain was a mistake, Delaware planter and lawmaker
John Dickinson claimed. "To rush into war at this time for
Wilderness beyond the River Mexicano, or on the remote waters
of the Missouri, would be . . . madness. . . ."[28]

7

Agent 13

*Can a man of your superior genius prefer a subordinate and
contracted position as the commander of the small and
insignificant army of the United States, to the glory of being
the founder of an empire—the liberator of so many millions of
his countrymen—the Washington of the West?
—Barón de Carondelet, Spanish Governor-General of
Louisiana, to Gen. James Wilkinson, U.S. Army*[1]

IT IS DIFFICULT to understand why James Wilkinson's
star seemed to shine undimmed through the administra-
tions of Washington, Adams, and Jefferson. His background was
notable for quirky and questionable activities. During the Revolution, as clothier-general under Washington in the Continental
Army, his performance had been lackluster at best. He became
embroiled in an insurrection attempt in November 1777 when
General Washington intercepted copies of letters between General Horatio Gates and General Thomas Conway, both serving
in the Continental Army. Gates had been a former English officer who defected to the patriot ranks in an effort to gain military

rank; Conway, an Irish immigrant, had been a former mercenary in the French army. The letters exposed their plot to unseat Washington at the head of the Continental Army and replace him with the ambitious Gates. When confronted, Gates lied to cover up the scheme, claiming it was all an attempt to ferret out a spy, who, he suggested, might even be in Washington's own camp. Seeing through the thin lie, Washington revealed that he had learned about it from James Wilkinson.

Actually, Wilkinson had been drunk in a tavern and had spilled the plot, which he was part of, to some officers loyal to Washington. They passed the information on to their commander, who was unaware of Wilkinson's involvement. Wilkinson turned on the elderly Gates, challenging him to a duel, which shocked Gates, as he had long been Wilkinson's mentor. The planned coup, known as the Conway Cabal, dissolved after it was revealed. In the interest of national unity, Washington let the matter drop. He promoted Wilkinson to brigadier general to repay him for supposedly busting the Cabal.[2]

After the war ended, Wilkinson married the Philadelphia heiress Ann Biddle and moved to Kentucky to launch a mercantile business on the new frontier. He opened a store in Louisville and with his in-laws' money purchased 12,550 acres of land. He realized that trade offered the greatest financial opportunity, but it was impossible to undermine Spanish control of the Mississippi, the critical river of commerce.

In 1786 the Spanish closed the Mississippi River to American products in an effort to force Americans on the frontier to align with Spain. James Wilkinson tried to turn the situation to his advantage by testing the Spanish and sending a flatboat of tobacco and hogs to New Orleans.[3] He realized that if he could monopolize American shipping on the Mississippi, he could make a fortune—as long as he was the only American allowed to do so. When his flatboat of trade products arrived, it was impounded by the Spanish. That led to a meeting with Spanish officials, including Governor Esteban Miró and his administrator, Martin Navarro, who asked Wilkinson for information about the status of things in Kentucky. He wrote a report for them, to which he added—with no suggestion from the Spanish—that he would just as soon become a Spanish citizen if necessary, in order to cement a potential future trade relationship. He claimed allegiance to the king of Spain, boldly asking for the exclusive right to operate American trade on the Mississippi River. And he sweetened the offer by promising to incite a revolt in Kentucky, which would lead to its secession from the United States and its becoming a Spanish state.[4]

Wilkinson knew he was committing treason when he wrote to Miró, noting, "I have committed secrets of an important nature such as would, were they divulged, destroy my fame and fortune forever."[5] The Spanish were surprised but accepted his help, allowing him to trade $75,000 worth of goods at New Orleans, thrilled with the prospect that Kentucky might soon become Spain's with no effort on their part.

Back in Kentucky, Wilkinson was a hero. He had opened the river trade—even though he was monopolizing it—and he promised independence and prosperity to backwoods settlers. As Kentucky was still part of Virginia, Wilkinson lobbied the Virginia legislature to let Kentucky form an independent republic, allied with Spain. His plans were now hardly secret. Foiling his carefully laid strategy to create a separate republic, however, in 1791 Kentucky joined the Union as a state. Wilkinson would have to look elsewhere to find his profits.

It was Wilkinson who exposed George Rogers Clark's alliance with Genet and their plans to take over the Mississippi region from Spain. When Wilkinson learned of it, he informed the Spanish officials in New Orleans, reassuring them he had already bribed the leaders in Clark's group. He may well have, because Clark's effort evaporated without a clear reason. Later Wilkinson told the Spanish he had spent $4,500 on bribes, for which they reimbursed him.[6] Clearly, he saw all other efforts to set up an independent empire in the West as a competition and a threat, and he did what he could to trounce such efforts. That meant he had to forge alliances with both frontiersmen and foreign governments: Hamilton had planned to work with Britain; George Rogers Clark and perhaps Jefferson had France; Wilkinson now had Spain. Time would tell.

Not until after the Spanish-American War in Cuba in 1898, when the Spanish archives at Havana were moved to Washington, D.C., did the historian I. J. Cox find records to prove Wilkinson's involvement as an undercover agent for Spain.[7] Among Cox's findings were records of payments to Wilkinson, a total of $32,000 in gold between 1790 and 1794. His official secret title was Agent 13. His Spanish connections had been rumored in Kentucky as early as 1788; by 1795 his connections were questioned even in the capital at Philadelphia. Washington did not confront him directly but sent U.S. government surveyor-general Andrew Ellicott to investigate Wilkinson. In 1798 Ellicott sent a letter to President Adams's administration, describing payments Wilkinson had received from Spain, but Secretary of State Timothy Pickering considered it an unsubstantiated rumor and did not pass the information to the president.[8]

When Washington asked Andrew Ellicott to investigate Wilkinson, Alexander Hamilton had suggested that Washington simply purchase Wilkinson's loyalty. Recognizing Wilkinson's true character by that time, Washington agreed to promote him to major general, to "feed his ambition, soothe his vanity," and appease his discontent.[9] For Washington it was critical to bind men from the frontier regions to the central government; otherwise the nation might split apart into minor fiefdoms. For that reason Wilkinson was valuable, because he was so very popular in the back country. Undoubtedly Jefferson understood him in a similar light. A year into his presidency, Jefferson received an anonymous letter from Kentucky, warning him that Wilkinson had been at the head of a plot to separate Kentucky from the Union.[10] He ignored it—after all, he had known about the plot for some time.

Gen. James Wilkinson knew the value of bribery firsthand, and when he promised to foment a rebellion in Kentucky he asked Spanish officials for a secret military commission, a pension, and enough guns to make it happen. He claimed the arms were necessary to protect settlers from Indians, and hinted that he might be forced to deal with Britain to get them. He passed along a list of Kentucky officials as well, advising the Spaniards to pay the Kentuckians bribes of between $500 and $1,000 a year.

AFTER the Louisiana Purchase in 1803, Jefferson was faced with the problem of governing the vast country west of the Mississippi, which had never been anticipated. In the Ohio country, Illinois, and Georgia, Indians were the most problematic presence. They continued to resist the Americans who took their lands, and pushing the Indians north or south only made matters worse. Jefferson decided that the new lands west of the Mississippi could serve as a vast camp where Indians could be sent.[11] There they could learn civilized ways at their own pace while their former lands could be settled safely by growing numbers of settlers—all of whom would vote the Republican ticket. Jefferson wrote to Pierre Dupont de Nemours that "our policy will be to form New Orleans, and the country on both sides of it on the Gulf of Mexico into a state; and as to all above that, to transplant our Indians into it, constituting them a Marechaussee [mounted constabulary] to prevent emigrants crossing the river, until we have filled up the vacant country on this side."[12] It would be relatively simple and would solve so many problems. With Indians at the border, Americans would not push farther west, beyond the reaches of government. Yet opening everything east of the Mississippi to white settlement would provide plenty of room for expansion.

Plans were being set for a major population resettlement program, but Jefferson had never seen the region firsthand. Would his scheme work? One of Meriwether Lewis's duties as he passed through St. Louis had been to examine the local situation and determine if the French residents of St. Louis would be amenable to Jefferson's plan to trade their holdings there for land east of the Mississippi. That would mean abandoning their homes to Indians, who would be relocated there by the government. Thus Lewis walked the streets of St. Louis, a town established in 1764 by emigrants from Canada and New Orleans. It was thriving on the river fur trade, with about a thousand residents made up of whites, free blacks, and slaves. "The advantages of such a [resettlement] policy has ever struck me as being of primary importance to the future prosperity of the Union," Lewis dutifully agreed. Yet, seeing it for himself, he realized how illogical and unworkable the plan was.[13] He told Jefferson that slavery was the crux—the French feared Americans meant to free their slaves. They would demand to remain as they were, simply to protect slavery.

While Jefferson and the rest of the nation wondered what to do with Louisiana, Wilkinson acted in his own interests. In February 1804 he wrote a paper, "Reflections on Louisiana," in response to a meeting with Vicente Folch, the Spanish governor of West Florida. Wilkinson suggested actions that Spain needed to take in order to remain powerful in North America in the wake of the Louisiana Purchase. He charged $20,000 for the information but was paid only a little more than half that amount. He advised that Lewis and Clark, then at Camp Dubois near St. Louis, be stopped from further exploration, and that Spain either retain the Floridas or trade them for land west of the Mississippi, to make Mexico safe from an "army of adventurers." He warned that the United States would have a post on the Pacific in five years. He added the suggestion that former American-turned-Spanish subject Daniel Boone be removed from his established home and salt works on the lower Missouri River. Wilkinson would not allow any American competitors, who were not under his control, into what he now viewed as his private turf.[14]

Jefferson meanwhile appointed Wilkinson to act as the first territorial governor for the new Louisiana acquisition; he arrived in St. Louis and began work in July 1805. Objecting to the appointment, critics questioned whether it was ethical to combine civil and military authority in the same individual. Jefferson responded that Louisiana was really a military station anyway. A military man who also acted as governor would be available to respond to any encroachments the Spanish might make.[15]

Ignoring Lewis's advice, Jefferson privately told Wilkinson to begin moving white residents of Louisiana, formerly French or Spanish citizens, to new locations east of the Mississippi River. The west side would be home to displaced Indians as their lands were sold.[16]

The job was nothing new to Wilkinson; he was experienced in dealing with boundaries and land problems. He had spent three years working directly for Jefferson on securing Indian land titles, to gain cessions of land for strategic roads and military posts.[17] He had run boundary lines, built roads between military posts, and established forts. He warned that the vast Western lands created a security threat and told the secretary of war that angry tribes would be stimulated by the British and Spanish to go to war with the United States.[18]

As governor, James Wilkinson could accomplish little in the way of gaining Indian allies or relocating Louisiana's citizenry across the river. Bypassing Wilkinson's official superior, the secretary of war, Jefferson and Wilkinson secretly sent letters back and forth about the depopulation effort. But the fur traders were well-established in a profitable location, and they refused to leave St. Louis.[19]

OUTSIDE OF his experience, why Wilkinson? What made Jefferson rely on him as commissioner of the southern Indians and as territorial governor and superintendent of Indian affairs in the Louisiana Territory? As a subordinate, Wilkinson was not to be trusted—he had tried to discredit Gen. Anthony Wayne as insane when he served under him, gaining him the appellation of "Mad" Anthony Wayne. He did the same to George Rogers Clark when serving under him. But from 1802 to 1806 he was Jefferson's right-hand man. His Indian experience had been "at the point of a gun," the historian Anthony F. C. Wallace points out.[20] Wallace writes, "Jefferson never wavered in his support of the general and afterward appointed him as an emissary to Spanish officials in Cuba. Eventually Wilkinson retired to Mexico and died there in 1825."[21]

Jefferson and Wilkinson worked closely together over a long period of time; they were both jealous of Washington and eager to place themselves at the center of the political scene. Both were political animals. And both were involved in the Corps of Discovery from its inception. As David Chandler notes, "The Lewis and Clark project was encrusted with politics."[22]

Thomas Jefferson had a history of connections with men who sought to shave off parts of the fledgling democracy and set up their own countries. Jefferson's close associate, Senator William Blount, a fellow Republican and former governor of Tennessee, had conspired with British agents to set up an independent state by seizing New Orleans. Jefferson was accused by some of having a part in it, but he sequestered himself at Monticello during Blount's treason hearings. Later Jefferson dismissed the charges against Blount, determining it was a state and not a federal matter, and should have been handled by Tennessee.[23] Jefferson was also heavily involved with the participants in Aaron Burr's scheme, which became known as the Burr Conspiracy. Burr and Wilkinson planned to foment secession in the West while invading Mexico, where they would set up an independent government based at New Orleans. Before Wilkinson revealed the scheme to the public, Jefferson had worked closely with the plotters.

Edmund Genet and André Michaux had tried to raise a volunteer American army to seize Louisiana and the Western states; George Rogers Clark and John Breckenridge were both involved in that failed scheme.[24] Jefferson, frustrated by the Federalists' opposition to the Louisiana Purchase, wrote to Breckenridge in

1803 that he could accept the secession of the Western states. He was frustrated by the Federalists' criticism and opposition to the Louisiana Purchase, but he was also the president of the United States. He wrote to Dr. Joseph Priestly in January 1804 that separating the nation into two sections, east and west, could be the right course to take: "Whether we remain in one confederacy, or form into Atlantic and Mississippi confederacies, I believe not very important to the happiness of either part. Those of the western confederacy will be as much our children & descendants as those of the eastern, and I feel myself as much identified with that country, in future time, as with this; and did I now foresee at some future day, yet I should feel the duty and the desire to promote the western interests as zealously as the eastern, doing all the good for both portions of our future family which should fall within my power." Without a pause, Jefferson continued by asking if Priestly had "seen the new work of Malthus on population? It is one of the ablest I have ever seen. Altho' his main object is to delineate the effects of redundancy of population, and to test the poor laws of England, & other palliations for that evil, several important questions in political economy, allied to his subject, are treated with a masterly hand."[25] Jefferson saw the vast uncultivated lands in North America as a protection against population limits. Malthusian environmental limits might well affect populations in Europe, he agreed, but America was a different story entirely.[26]

Wallace believes Jefferson may very well have considered creating "a new, free, western nation built upon Republican principles" if the Federalists had created a powerful central government, which Jefferson abhorred. In that case Jefferson "may have looked upon Wilkinson, with all his faults, indeed precisely because of his faults, as the potential commander of the military force needed to defend the independence of the trans-Appalachian Republic from the Federalist Army that would inevitably be sent to suppress it." Would it be the Whiskey Rebellion all over again? If so, Jefferson would be ready, with a general and an army.[27]

A PERPETUAL SELF-STARTER, Wilkinson sent expeditions of his own into the West, privately financing a venture to follow Lewis and Clark upriver. He wrote to Secretary of War Henry Dearborn on September 8, 1805, to say that "I have equipt a Perogue out of my small private means, not with any view to self interest, to ascend the Missouri and enter the River Piere Jaune, or Yellow Stone, called by the natives, Unicorn River, the same by which Captain Lewis and I expect to return and which my informants tell me is filled with wonders. This Party will not get back before the Summer of 1807—They are natives of this Town, and are just able to give us course and distance, with the names and populations of the Indian nations and to bring back with them Specimens of the natural products."

"What happened to this expedition, if it developed, is not known," Donald Jackson speculates. "There are fascinating reports of white men on the upper Missouri at this time, unaffiliated with Lewis and Clark."[28] There was "fragmentary evidence of this expedition or another unidentified one, and its contacts with British travelers, in David Thompson's narrative regarding forty-two Americans on the affluents of the Columbia."[29]

Wilkinson wrote to Dearborn about another private venture: he equipped "a bold adventurer," Captain John McClallen, who had gone upriver, planning to continue up the Platte to establish trade with the Pawnees. Lewis and Clark in fact met McClallen as they were descending the lower Missouri River in

September 1806. He told them he was "on rather a speculative expedition to the confines of New Spain, with the view to entroduce a trade with those people."[30]

While Wilkinson busied himself by sending out secret ventures, Jefferson pressed Congress for a war with Spain. In December 1805 he sent a letter to Congress detailing grievances and depredations against Americans living along the borders. He urged Congress to allow him to dip into the Treasury to respond with force, if necessary, to prevent Spanish reinforcements along the border. He wanted to fortify the U.S. naval presence in the Gulf of Mexico too, and asked that any Spanish build-up of posts in Louisiana be "opposed by force."[31] His State of the Union address to Congress that month noted that "with Spain our negotiations for a settlement of differences have not had a satisfactory issue. . . . Propositions for adjusting amicably the boundaries of Louisiana have not been acceded to . . . our citizens have been seized and their property plundered in the very parts of the former [territory] which had been actually delivered up by Spain, and this by the regular officers and soldiers of that Government. I have therefore found it necessary at length to give orders to our troops on that frontier to be in readiness to protect our citizens, and to repel by arms any similar aggressions in future." Jefferson estimated there were about 300,000 young men, potential recruits who could be called to serve in a militia, and he called for the revival of an active militia. He also advised building warships, moving defenses into port cities, and cracking down on privateers in the Gulf of Mexico.[32]

Jefferson did not mention that the Corps of Discovery, a U.S. detachment of armed and trained military men, was somewhere in the west, on land that belonged to Spain. The only reference to the Lewis and Clark expedition was that he had no news from beyond the Mississippi River. "A state of our progress in exploring the principle [sic] rivers of that country, and of the information respecting them hitherto obtained, will be communicated so soon as we shall receive some further relations which we have reason shortly to expect."[33] Certainly if news came that Lewis and his party had been tragically murdered by Spanish forces, Congress would respond as a match to tinder.

After Lewis and Clark departed upriver, and Wilkinson warned the Spanish about them, the general attempted to enter the fur trade as a private businessman, outfitting a few trade expeditions to test the Indian market. Those ventures are understandable, but another venture at the same time has been difficult for historians to explain: the haphazard, seemingly ill-designed forays by Lt. Zebulon Montgomery Pike. "Wilkinson's exact purpose in sending Pike into Mexico, like many other shadowy dealings of this double agent, continues to elude full explanation," the historian David Weber notes.[34] Pike was sent directly into Spanish territory, with no attempt to be clandestine. In fact he appeared to seek the attention of the Spanish.

In 1805 Wilkinson sent young Lieutenant Pike and twenty men up the Mississippi River, only months behind Lewis and Clark. Perhaps he sent Pike to scout Lewis and Clark's route, to see if they had actually gone up the Missouri or if they (and Jefferson) had surreptitiously sent the party up the Mississippi, on a venture to which Wilkinson was not privy. Pike wintered in Minnesota and returned in the spring. Wilkinson then sent him on another trek that spring, overland to the Red River and down to Natchitoches, directly into Spanish holdings.

Pike's trips were military in nature, and not secret. Wilkinson put the plans together and alerted the War Department beforehand. Lieutenant Pike, with little forethought or planning, his men clad only in thin summer uniforms, left St. Louis on July 15, 1806. As he had with Lewis and Clark's expedition, Wilkinson quickly alerted the Spanish that Pike was on his way into their territory. On this venture, Wilkinson's son, Lt. James B. Wilkinson, Jr., went along too.[35] Why he outfitted and sent one of his most trusted men, along with his son, on an unexplainable foray, then contacted the Spaniards about it, is confusing. It appears he wanted the party to be captured by Spain so that he and Jefferson would finally have a significant frontier incident which they could use to incite war. Sending his son along meant that Wilkinson would have a firsthand reporter, someone who could elaborate on any Spanish depredations and would be loyal to his father.

Pike's group visited a Pawnee village on the Republican River, just inside present-day Nebraska. The Pawnees were Spanish allies and told Pike that a large group of Spanish troops had been there a few days earlier, led by Lt. Facundo Melgares. Pike believed they were looking for him, so he began following the Melgares party up to the Rockies, where he promptly got lost. The Melgares attachment was actually looking for Lewis and Clark, who were then returning from the Pacific.[36]

From today's vantage point, it is easy to read Pike's account, knowing that Wilkinson was a consummate conniver, and believe that Pike was never actually lost but only pretending to be. He had told Wilkinson that if the Spanish stopped him he would pretend to be lost. Donald Jackson believes "Pike became really lost, not once but three times." Nevertheless it is clear that Pike was not trying to avoid encountering Spanish military units; he apparently *hoped* to meet up with them. As a spy for Wilkinson— which is exactly what Pike was—he would have wanted to know the Spanish military strength in the region, and the location of their troops.[37] Eventually, in February 1807, a Spanish patrol

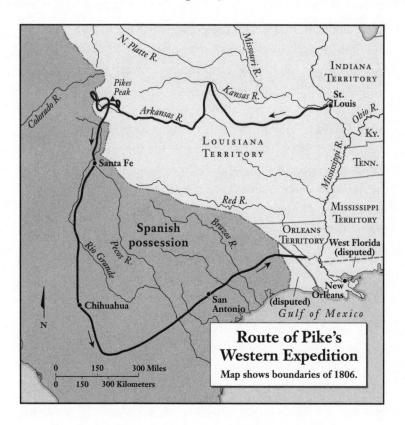

Route of Pike's Western Expedition
Map shows boundaries of 1806.

from Santa Fe discovered Pike, who had built a stockade and was flying a U.S. flag, near the Rio Grande. Certainly making every effort to be visible, Pike told them he thought he was on the Red River. They took him and his men to see the governor in Chihuahua, where he was detained and released in June 1807.[38]

While Pike was wandering the Rockies, his men suffering frostbite and worse, and while Jefferson was urging more gunships along the Gulf, Meriwether Lewis and his expeditionary force reached the end of their journey. The Corps arrived on the Pacific Coast in early November and exulted in its goal realized:

"the delightful prospect of the ocean—that ocean, the object of all our labors, the reward of all our anxieties." The trip had been harrowing and physically challenging, but all had gone well. Only one man had died, and that had been early on, from appendicitis. Patrick Gass, one of the younger members, wrote in his diary, "We are now at the end of our voyage, which has been completely accomplished according to the intention of the expedition, the object of which was to discover a passage by the way of the Missouri and Columbia rivers to the Pacific ocean; notwithstanding the difficulties, privations and dangers, which we had to encounter, endure and surmount."[39] Now the group was ready to return home.

As Gass was writing, Meriwether Lewis had gone "to see if any white people were to be found." The Indians they met "informed us that in two days we would come to two ships with white people in them," Gass wrote. He noted that "the Indians here have a great deal of new cloth among them, and other articles which they got from these ships."[40] Clark described Indians at the mouth of the Columbia River, dressed in "scarlet & blue blankets, sailor's jackets & trousers, shirts & hats." They carried "war-axes, spears, bows & arrows, or muskets & pistols with tin powder-flasks."[41] It appeared certain that the expedition would soon encounter white traders; their effects were everywhere. They encountered some Indians who spoke a few English words and who told of trading with a "Mr. Haley." One of the Clatsop Indians from the region was a young man about twenty-five years old, who had red hair and a light, freckled complexion, but who did not speak English.[42]

Along the Columbia, the significance to the coastal people of white trade was obvious. The Indians told Lewis that ships arrived in April and October to trade guns and ammunitions, kettles, blankets, copper and brass plates, knives, tobacco, fish hooks, and lots of ready-made clothing. Lewis assumed the traders were either English or American, because the Indians used English words and phrases such as "musket," "powder," "shot," "knife," "damned rascal," and "son of a bitch." But he could not determine whether the ships came down from Nootka Sound or elsewhere on the coast, or directly from the United States or Britain.[43] When asked where the ships went, the Indians pointed to the southwest, which probably meant they did not go to Nootka, which lay to the north. Lewis figured there must be an island off to the southwest, and indeed the Sandwich Islands (Hawaii) were the usual next port of call. Certainly Lewis was familiar with Cook's travels in the Pacific and would have already read about his discovery of the Sandwich Islands, which Cook had named.

The natives discussed the better-known traders who had arrived on the coast, telling about one named Moore who had come with three cows on ship, and continued north. That may have indicated a white settlement farther up the coast. The Indians recited a list of favorite traders who came frequently in three- or four-masted ships: Youens, Tallamon, Callalamet (who they described as having a wooden leg), Swipton, Moore, Mackey, Washington, Mesship, Davidson, Jackson, Bolch, and Skelley (who had only one eye and had not been back in a few years).[44]

It appeared that the trading season was over; a ship had just left the area days before the white men arrived. They would now have to wait until spring. Clark wrote in November that they hoped to meet some ships that were "expected in about three months, and from which we may procure a fresh supply of trinkets for our route homeward."[45]

The question that piques the greatest interest in the story of

Lewis and Clark's expedition trip to the Pacific is, why was there no ship to meet them? Historians have puzzled over it, drawing few conclusions. Certainly the Pacific coast was a hub of trade activity; ships had been in and out of the area for years. Captain Charles Bishop, on the British ship *Ruby*, had even stayed long enough to plant vegetable gardens on an island at the mouth of the Columbia, in 1795 and 1796, harvesting potatoes, radishes, and beans—a striking example of how well traveled the region had become.[46]

Lewis and Clark scholar Elliott Coues questions Jefferson's actions in not arranging a ship to meet the party. He notes that only a few years later, John Jacob Astor sent a party of U.S. fur traders overland and arranged for a ship to meet them on the coast. As president, Jefferson could have just as easily accommodated Lewis and Clark. Coues writes, "One naturally wonders why President Jefferson did not take the same care of his Expedition. The advantage of such an arrangement is so self-evident, that there must have been some strong reason why it was not made. It could not have been overlooked; it must have been discussed, and rejected."[47] But why? Perhaps, Coues speculates, an American ship would have alerted Spain to the expedition, and Jefferson sought to downplay incursions on Spanish territory by not sending a ship through the Pacific where they would have seen it. But that does not make much sense, because American trading ships had been plying the northwest coast since before the Nootka affair. Several American ships in the Pacific were engaged in whale fishing at that time too.

Perhaps Jefferson did not really expect Lewis to make it to the Pacific. Perhaps Jefferson did not even *want* Lewis to arrive on the Pacific coast. What he may have wanted, and enlisted Wilkinson to obtain, was a martyr. If Lewis and his party had been captured or killed by Spain or her Indian allies, Jefferson could have used the incident to reinforce his desire to take Florida and Texas.

Lewis was likable, but to Jefferson he could have been expendable, as were many who crossed his path. Wilkinson's blatant alerts to the Spanish officials, telling them to capture Lewis, were made early on, before the expedition even got under way. A Spanish capture of Lewis then, near St. Louis, would have been invaluable for public relations. But it did not happen. No one knew where Lewis and Clark were, and after a few months, few expected them to return. Jefferson made no plans for their return, prepared no potential projects related to establishing a U.S. presence on the Pacific coast. Lewis had fully expected a ship to provide for his return, as well as to provide much needed supplies. But none arrived. Nevertheless Lewis was nothing if not idealistic and loyal to the president. Something must have interfered or gone wrong, he thought. He may have thought the Federalists or the British, both of whom he hated, had skewered Jefferson's plans. There was nothing to do but return overland. And, though it is evident from remarks in his diary that on the return he was short-tempered with Indians they met, and not as enthusiastic about what he was seeing, he "proceeded on."

ON ARRIVING at the coast, the Corps camped on the north side of the Columbia River, in what is today Washington State, but the site was difficult. It rained constantly, and there was a dearth of game to hunt. Meat and salt were necessary for the winter, and neither was available. After a bit of scouting and advice from local natives, the group took a vote and headed across the river, to winter at a site they named Fort Clatsop.

It was rainy, wet, and miserable. Private Gass complained in his diary about ticks and flies, along with freezing weather and snow. They had only game to eat, which spoiled easily in the damp air, and no salt. Spirits sank with each day that passed without news of a ship in the area. There would be no return by sea, no immediate respite from trail life, and, most disappointing, no fresh supplies. By mid-January the men were at work fleshing hides to make moccasins, "a laborious business, but we have no alternative in this part of the country," Gass wrote.[48] The moccasins, a sort of handmade currency, enabled them to trade with neighboring Indians for vital food supplies.

By late March the men had to decide whether to wait for a ship, which might arrive soon, or start back upriver and overland. Having waited for months, Lewis decided to turn back overland, all together. He justified his decision in his journal, noting that the group was too small to spare a few men to go back by sea, and that if they all went overland they might get home sooner than by ship because a trading ship would remain on the coast for the summer, then might not go directly to the United States.[49] They had waited as long as they could, subsisting on elk meat from a herd that wintered nearby. By the end of winter the men had made new hide clothing and repaired some equipment. But most were extremely sick, the sickest they had been since leaving the Wood River camp along the Mississippi, suffering from diarrhea, syphilis, lung infections, and dietary deficiencies. Lewis treated them according to medical practice of the time—bloodletting and doses of mercury—but they were in terrible shape. He knew they had only three days' supply of dried meat for emergencies. By March 5, when the hunters concluded that the elk had moved upland with the coming of spring, Lewis realized, "We must make up our minds to start soon, ascend the river slowly, endeavoring to find subsistence on the way. . . ."[50] His men were sick and dying, without proper food "which we have it not in our power to procure," Lewis lamented[51] He had to get them out of camp and upriver—or they might all die before a ship ever arrived.

As they pushed off, Lewis faced another problem linked to his failure to locate a trade ship: he had no stock of trade goods, vital to enlisting native support on the trip home. He still carried Jefferson's letter of credit, now worthless. An ample supply of trade items would have made "a much more comfortable homeward-bound journey," Lewis noted.[52] As it was, the men departed Fort Clatsop carrying the only trading stock they had left—338 pairs of handmade elkskin moccasins.[53]

8

The Burr Conspiracy

What was treason in me thirty years ago is patriotism now.
—Aaron Burr, living in obscurity, after Sam Houston defeated
Mexican forces in 1836 and established the Republic of Texas[1]

WHILE Meriwether Lewis and William Clark and their party were wondering how they would fare getting back to the United States, another series of events was unfolding which remain both fascinating and puzzling to historians today. Aaron Burr, former vice president with Jefferson while Lewis was Jefferson's secretary, had been formulating the strangest political move in American history, known as the Burr Conspiracy. Burr, a talented and popular politician, went from American hero to consummate villain during the period Lewis and Clark were in the West. The downfall began in 1804 when Burr killed Alexander Hamilton in a personal duel.

Hamilton, born on the sugar island of Nevis in the Caribbean, grew up penniless (and fatherless), and during the Revolutionary War found a mentor in George Washington. When Washington became president in 1789, he appointed

Hamilton secretary of the treasury. He served until 1795, then returned to a successful law practice in New York. In 1798 he developed ambitions to do more. It was an era thick with filibusters—insurrectionist efforts aimed at taking over another country's domain and installing oneself in a place of power. Others, such as John Sevier, William Blount, Elijah Clarke, and much later even Sam Houston and John C. Frémont set out on filibusters of their own in the West. Politics was a seedbed for personal ambition in the period after the American Revolution, and while the nation's independence offered opportunity, so too did it create conspiracy and intrigue. Men like Jefferson, Burr, and Hamilton, and lesser-knowns like James Wilkinson, all sought to make the most of the potential opportunities available in the newly created nation. In an era before the rise of political parties, men's ambitions often turned to gathering a group of followers. Yet followers were wont to look for what a leader could offer them in exchange for loyalty and support. Filibusters offered what everyone on the crowded frontiers wanted: free land. One's national affiliation could be fairly flexible.

As he sought to design a political future for himself, Hamilton began to speculate on taking the rest of the continent away from Spain. In 1800, with Jefferson as president, Hamilton and the Federalists found themselves out of power. Hamilton's declining political fortunes promised to revive with a new start in the West. He planned to send an army down the Mississippi River to meet a waiting British fleet at sea. From there they would wrest New Orleans from Spain and advance to take all of Mexico.[2] We may never know if he sought Spanish territory for the nation, as a springboard into elected office, or if he merely wanted his own fiefdom. Hamilton's effort collapsed, largely because of his own untimely death at the hands of his longtime antagonist Aaron Burr, in a duel between the two on July 11, 1804. On that day Lewis and Clark and party were already more than 520 miles up the Missouri into northeastern Kansas.[3]

Burr succeeded Hamilton as a filibuster-minded politician, with a two-stage plan. He and his friends planned to set up a colony on private tracts of land that straddled the Louisiana-Arkansas border within the United States. Then, after instigating war with Spain, at the outbreak of fighting Burr and his minions would take over Texas, then move on to conquer Mexico.[4] By 1805 Burr's ambitions for the West were widely known. Like Hamilton, he was also an adversary of Thomas Jefferson, who viewed him as a threat because Burr was a politically popular war hero. Not a landed Virginian, Burr did not fit with Jefferson's plan to run the government with a succession of Virginia planters.

Although Burr was vice president during Jefferson's presidency, at the time the two were rivals rather than colleagues. In the 1800 election the Republicans had understood Jefferson would be at the top of the ticket because he could win the electoral votes of the Southern states, where the slave population was manipulated to gain electoral votes. Each slave counted as three-fifths of a person, boosting population figures for House representation. In New York State, however, Burr appealed to free black voters because he was an adamant abolitionist. Thus Burr was added to the ticket because, as a Republican in largely Federalist territory, he could deliver New York's electoral votes.[5] Votes were not assigned to either office—electors cast votes for the two candidates. It was expected that the chosen candidate would prevail, and the runner-up would become the vice president. But in 1800 Burr won as many electoral votes as Jefferson, meaning they were tied for the presidency. The tie went to the House of Representatives and a standoff began. Eventually, due to political promises and much wrangling, Jefferson won the presidency from Burr by one vote, on the thirty-sixth ballot. Jefferson had by no means received a mandate.

Burr, of average height and slight build, had been a Revolutionary War hero. (Jefferson was not, having remained in Virginia as governor and done such a poor job that he was later castigated by the Virginia legislature.) He was also popular among Federalists; in fact, had he chosen to switch parties he might have been guaranteed the presidency in the face-off with Jefferson in 1800. He was charming and popular, as well as bipolar, inclined to "hypo" (as he called it) or to fits of depression.[6] Confronting the wily and grudging Thomas Jefferson, he would vacillate between the two conditions for the next four years.

Aside from Jefferson's personal animosity toward Burr, the Louisiana Purchase itself divided political and national interests. The Federalists, concentrated on the New England seaboard, saw the 1803 purchase as a sellout to their interests. They profited by sea trade with Great Britain, the world's commercial powerhouse, and saw Jefferson's deal as bolstering Napoleon's war machine against Britain. The payments for Louisiana were to come from trade duties paid by New England merchants, while the benefits suited only agricultural interests—Southern plantation interests in particular.

Jefferson idealized the nation's yeoman farmers, who indeed supported him wholeheartedly because the addition of thousands of Western acres promised the opportunity for land ownership for nearly everyone. They voted for Jefferson and his Republicans because they thought he would open Western lands to them. But for New Englanders, the West was only a divisive issue that promised to demolish their carefully constructed trade world.

They argued that France might never even honor the purchase agreement, and that the paltry United States Army would then be forced to fight France over Louisiana.

Problematic too was Jefferson's plan to govern the new region, a plan that was completely undemocratic. The new government and the president would rule there by executive order. In the president's scheme there were no voters, no legislature, no trial by jury. The residents would be taxed without their consent. It entirely contradicted the ideals of the recently fought Revolution. The region would have slavery, though no Africans could be imported: slaves would be sold from existing states into the fields of the West. Under the Constitution, all states would be prohibited from importing foreign slaves by 1808, but most states had already prohibited the entry of African slaves.[7] With no competition from importers, established planters prospered by supplying slaves to the interior.

New England's Federalists were more attuned to Britain and favored manumission as well as continued free trade in the West Indies. Jefferson and France both abhorred the recent slave revolts in Haiti and intended to restore slavery to Haiti as soon as possible. Jeffersonians clung to an alliance with France in an effort to save slavery, but they needed more—they needed new lands. Virginia planters were struggling with worn-out soil, their only export becoming more and more that of slaves to fresh lands being cultivated for cotton. "Virginia was the nation's principal exporter of slaves," the historian Roger Kennedy explains.[8]

Cotton was becoming king in the South, following the perfection of the cotton gin, which breathed new life into cotton farming because it could process the kind of cotton grown at higher elevations. This meant that new lands could be put into cotton, necessitating new slaves to do the work. Expanding plantation agriculture would expand slavery, and it was the only solution for dwindling production on older farms. When the steam engine was adapted to power Eli Whitney's cotton gin, cotton production soared. Prices for cotton rose too, due to the Napoleonic Wars, which both created larger markets for American exports and devastated cotton production in Egypt. As the gin became more popular, so did cotton cultivation, a labor-intensive crop. Even Jefferson's Indian policy took King Cotton into account. His plan centered on removing Native Americans who stood in the way of plantation agriculture.[9] As a market for slaves, Jefferson would personally find the West to be just about the only way to redeem his own flagging fortunes.

In the 1804 election Jefferson unceremoniously dumped Aaron Burr from the ticket, replacing him with George Clinton. In light of Burr's loss of popularity among New Yorkers following his duel with Hamilton, he was less useful than before. He was also a political threat to Jefferson, which the aging Clinton never would be. Watching his personal political future crumble, Burr looked for opportunity in the West like any other anxious American.

In May 1805 Burr traveled to St. Louis, where he met with General Wilkinson. It is not clear whether the ultimate plan was concocted by Burr or Wilkinson alone, or as co-conspirators, but the two of them worked out a scheme to invade Mexico. Wilkinson provided maps drawn by Philip Nolan and accounts written by Zebulon Pike (who at that moment was somewhere between the Colorado Rockies and Santa Fe, hoping to catch the attention of Spaniards). Later Wilkinson would attempt to clear his name by denouncing Burr, but in 1805 the two eagerly held clandestine discussions about the Western lands.[10] In November of that same year, Burr met for two hours with Jefferson in Washington City. Later Burr told others that he had explained his plans to the president and that they were met with "complacency." By then, Burr was ready to go to war with Mexico.

Weeks later, in December 1805, Jefferson sent a speech to Congress declaring his readiness to go to war with Spain, claiming Spanish troops had invaded American territory, seizing American citizens and their property. The incursions were across boundaries that had been relocated in February 1804, when the president claimed Spanish West Florida.

Burr had a large following among Westerners. While a senator, he had led the effort to bring Tennessee into the Union as the sixteenth state. He had also worked with Federalists who considered seceding to create a Northeast confederacy. In New Hampshire, Massachusetts, and Connecticut such a move appeared the only way to resist the rising tide of Jeffersonian power, the only way to counter the impact of the Louisiana Purchase on the nation's balance of power. To a region that relied on trade with England, Jefferson's tilt toward France was vexing.[11] But secession was a serious matter. At the time it appeared to depend upon a suitable foreign alliance, or at the least foreign funding.

The prospect of Mexico to the south and west, rather than French-owned Louisiana as a buffer, was worrisome to slave interests. France was pro-slavery; in fact, many French residents of Louisiana held slaves and worried they might lose them once the region was transferred to the United States. Spain, however, was a different matter. It had allowed Florida to become a runaway slave haven since 1687, when Spain inaugurated a policy designed to subvert British colonies in North America by offering freedom to slaves. If they fled on an underground railroad to Spanish Florida or Spanish Louisiana, they were to receive freedom, land, and, of course, Catholicism.[12] Beyond was Mexico, where Spain envisioned a slavery-free society. So disregarding Burr, the prospect of Mexico to the west as a haven for runaway slaves was chilling to Jeffersonian Virginians and cotton promoters.

In the summer of 1805 newspapers across the country as well as in England and Mexico carried stories about Burr's alleged plans as he made a tour of the West. In August 1805 the Philadelphia Federalist newspaper, the *Gazette of the United States*, questioned Burr's intentions. Word had circulated that Burr planned to undertake a major effort to "liberate" the West; it was said he would command ten thousand Kentuckians, three thousand Tennesseans, between eight and ten thousand militia from Louisiana, and five thousand slaves who would be given their freedom.[13] Burr's plans included the founding of an abolitionist colony on land he had purchased in the center of the most promising new cotton lands, along the Ouachita River.

At first Spanish officials thought Burr, as the former vice president in the Jefferson administration, was working on a government-sponsored effort to expand national boundaries. That was a threat. Some in the Spanish leadership saw it differently, however—Burr's plan might eventually aid Spanish interests. After meeting with Burr, Yrujo wrote to Cevallos that "Spain would view with extreme satisfaction the dismemberment of the colossal power which was growing up at the very gates of her most precious and important colonies."

Spanish officials working within the colonial bureaucracy of New Spain were from a variety of backgrounds: Irish immigrants fleeing Britain's hostilities, discontented Creoles, and ambitious *peninsulares*, born in Spain and seeking personal success in the colonial empire. They were becoming increasingly restless with the Spanish court. Burr counted on their willingness to work with Americans—if necessary on a joint effort—to liberate Mexico from Spain. Burr needed money, however, and offered to sell his services to Spain, which Yrujo advised the king to accept.[14] Yrujo believed that Burr's plan was to divide the Union, something which would benefit Spain's position. A separated America would be no threat, in fact the disaffected Western residents might be entreated to align themselves with Spain. The governor in West Florida, Vicente Folch, prepared to support American insurgents if they tried to separate from the Union.[15] Still, Spain would not be duped with a plan that sounded too good to be true, and Yrujo warned Spanish officials in the provinces to be on guard against a surprise attack by Americans.

Burr, consummate political thinker, had an alternative plan: unknown to the Spanish, he was also working on British support for his scheme. He spent nearly two years secretly lobbying British government interests for money, but to no avail.[16] When Spanish forces built up reinforcements at the northern frontier, the British suspected that Spain was joining with Burr to divide the United States.

Eventually Spanish officials realized that Burr intended to move on their holdings, but they expected him to dismember the Union first, before trying to move on Mexico. They may have believed they had plenty of time to watch developments in the Western states, intervening when it served their interests. Yrujo wrote to Cevallos in 1806, describing the situation: "There is in this country an infinite number of adventurers, without property, full of ambition, and ready to unite at once under the standard of a revolution which promises to better their situation."[17] Clearly that applied to both Mexico's disaffected subjects as well as those in Louisiana and the Western states. Informants told Spanish officials that Burr intended to take over Washington City, removing the president, vice president, and president of the Senate, then take the money from Washington banks and go on to New Orleans where he and his followers would declare independence.

It was in Spain's interest to let the unstable coalition of states squabble among themselves, and split as they might. In October 1806 Vicente Folch, governor of West Florida, wrote to the viceroy of Mexico, José de Iturrigaray, "You have already been informed of the project to revolutionize Mexico. This enterprise has not been lost sight of, and seems to be stronger than ever. According to the plan, if the weather permits, in February or March ten thousand Kentuckians, three thousand regular troops, eight or ten thousand militia from Louisiana who will be forced to go, will march for Mexico. They will raise a corps of five thousand blacks, who will be taken from the plantations and declared free. This will make an army of from twenty-eight to thirty-thousand men; five thousand will be reserved for the city of New Orleans. Baton Rouge and Pensacola will probably be the first taken . . . after that, Natchitoches will be the point for the reunion. Part of the army will be embarked to land at the Rio Grande. The pretext for this expedition is afforded by the presence of the Spanish troops at Adayes. Congress will act only on the defensive, but if once these troops are united they will march toward Mexico with great proclamations."[18] From Mexico's angle, things might become very uncertain.

IN MAY 1806 Secretary of War Henry Dearborn ordered Wilkinson to hurry to New Orleans to oversee the tense military situation there. But Wilkinson waited in St. Louis for three months before doing so. The historian Walter Flavius McCaleb writes, "His procrastination was deliberate, and could have been for no other purpose than to await the development of the conspiracy." Indeed, Wilkinson advised Burr that he would be ready before him.[19]

On April 9, 1806, Captain-General of the Internal Provinces of New Spain, Nemesio Salcedo, ordered six hundred Spanish militia to defend Texas from American attack, in response to U.S. forces moving across the Arroyo Hondo. Salcedo wrote to Governor Antonio Cordero that month: "Ever since France sold Louisiana to the United States, nothing has been left undone to extend the limits into the Spanish possessions of the Missouri and Arkansas, and to secure the twenty-two leagues of land lying between the Arroyo Hondo and the Sabine, the former of which marks the boundary of Louisiana as the Americans well know. They are also massing troops without question of expense to hold by force their spoils. They are also intriguing with the Indians, have built a storehouse at Natchitoches and have filled it with gifts for them. It has not been possible for us to oppose them in force, but in order to counteract their influence among the Indians I have dispatched expeditions to the various tribes, our dependencies—*some to the far Northwest*."[20] That expedition was the third attempt Spanish forces had made to arrest or stop Lewis and Clark.

Following up, Governor Cordero sent out emissaries on April 21 to meet with the various Indian tribes in Texas, warning them of the Burr plot. Spain figured it was an official or at least government-sanctioned plan. The viceroy sent all available troops forward within weeks.[21] In response to the Spanish build-up, Jefferson quickly ordered Secretary of War Dearborn to send six warships to New Orleans and three to Lake Pontchartrain, north of the city. Troops were to fortify New Orleans, and militia were ordered to be ready to seize Mobile or Pensacola. "These orders are to be carried out with as little noise as possible," Jefferson wrote.[22]

That summer of 1806 the Texas border crackled with conflict. Jefferson sent troops to the Texas-Louisiana border and Nemesio Salcedo ordered Lt. Col. Simón de Herrera to move twelve hundred men into east Texas to fend off possible U.S. incursions. General Wilkinson had been sent from St. Louis southward with American forces. Wilkinson claimed the odds were against him—"I have two Spanish Governors opposed to me, Herrera and Cordero, of whom and their two thousand men, I shall with less than twelve hundred give a good account."[23] Herrera, a man of "pride and spirit" according to Wilkinson, vowed to fight for Spain's rightful territory. Both men appeared to bluster more than battle.[24] Facing off, yet neither one ready to start a war, Herrera and Wilkinson met and worked out the Neutral Ground Treaty, leaving a swath of no-man's-land between the two countries.[25] It was not a treaty between nations but an agreement between two fighting forces, and oddly an agreement that Wilkinson, as a Spanish agent as well as head of the American forces, made with himself. Herrera moved his forces out of Bayou Pierre and west of the Sabine River, completely dissolving the near war.

The truce was not driven by popular opinion in the West, where Louisiana residents were eager to fight Spain. When a call for militia volunteers went out, men eagerly signed up. One call for 100 men was met with 215 volunteers. The people were chafing to fight Spaniards, but Wilkinson was dragging his feet, taking two weeks to make the three-day trip to army headquarters in Natchitoches.

The Neutral Ground Treaty was Wilkinson's response to the failure of Aaron Burr's efforts as well as a way to stop the forward motion of war with Spain. Burr and Wilkinson had met several times, and while their meetings were clandestine, they most likely were plotting to invade Mexico. Many felt at the time—and do today—that the two planned to separate Louisiana and the Western states from the union and create a separate country. While Wilkinson was busy facing off with Herrera's forces along the Sabine (or pretending to), Burr notified Wilkinson that their plan had collapsed. In response, possibly to protect himself, Wilkinson turned on Burr, sending a letter alerting Jefferson to his "discovery" of Burr's plans.

IN JULY 1806 the newspaper *Western World* began publication in Frankfort, Kentucky, for the purpose of publicizing what was becoming known as the "Burr Conspiracy" plot. The newspaper launched scathing and vindictive attacks on General Wilkinson, accusing him of being party to Burr's plot, and openly discussing his being in the employ of Spanish agents. The *World* faded away just weeks after Burr was tried in Kentucky, but for months it discussed the conspiracy, saying the plot had become an effort to align Western states in a move to secede. Word filtered east that five thousand Western men had taken up arms against the government; the public began to pay attention.[26]

On September 4, 1806, Burr arrived in Cincinnati, then went on to Lexington and to Tennessee, where he met with Andrew Jackson, who was ready to lead men forward. The region was ablaze with excitement over the pending Spanish war. "Every militiaman in the West was furbishing his accoutrements and awaiting the summons to the field," one account reported. Jackson toasted Burr at a public dinner in Nashville on September 27, saying, "Millions for defense; not one cent for tribute."[27]

Within a month Andrew Jackson had stirred up the Tennessee militia with newspaper announcements that Spanish forces were camped on U.S. territory, had captured U.S. citizens, and had forced a government exploring party (Pike's) to return from the Red River. He urged the militia to be prepared, then wrote to President Jefferson, offering to be the first volunteer for the coming war with Spain.[28] Jefferson evaded Jackson's offer, however, and did not tell him that he had just abandoned the war build-up in the West and that Wilkinson had halted along the Sabine River, waiting for a truce.[29]

That same September, jut a few days before Jackson jubilantly toasted Burr in Nashville, Meriwether Lewis and his party returned to St. Louis from their long journey to the Pacific. Lewis wrote to Jefferson on September 23, alerting him to the party's safe return. The nation was surprised and delighted that Lewis and Clark had come back from the Pacific, but public interest soon focused elsewhere. A reported conspiracy by the former vice president to separate the nation and attack a neighboring country was riveting the nation's attention.

AS THE STORY about Aaron Burr's plan to instigate a rebellion in the Western states followed by an invasion of Mexico made its way into the newspapers, a public outcry ensued. While the project had been public knowledge in the backcountry, Eastern readers were shocked. James Wilkinson acted quickly to protect himself. He wrote to Jefferson on October 20, 1806, warning the president that a large-scale treasonous plot had been exposed, but he refrained from naming Burr.[30] As the public grew more agitated by the news, Jefferson acted to distance himself from both Burr and Wilkinson and any hint of collusion with the pair. He ordered Wilkinson to cease any military efforts against Spain and quickly ended all moves toward war. He turned his full power toward gaining a conviction and execution of Burr for treason.

On November 25, 1806, a federal grand jury met in Kentucky to investigate Burr's conduct. He was quickly vindicated, much to Jefferson's dismay. In reaction, Jefferson promptly removed the prosecuting attorney from his position in the wake of his poor showing against Burr.[31] He now turned the full power of the presidency against Burr, once his own vice president. Jefferson charged Burr with planning an expedition against Spain for the purpose of seizing its possessions, thereby violating the Neutrality Act of 1794, a misdemeanor. He also levied a second charge against Burr for treason—a hanging offense.

Burr was tried for treason at Frankfort, Kentucky, and the *World* gave it full treatment, sensationalizing rumors as well as events. "The project of Colonel Burr is doubtless of the most extensive nature, and if accomplished will not only affect the interests of the Western country, but of the known world," the editor crowed. "A revolution in the Spanish provinces of North America will speedily, when aided by Miranda, lead to one in South America, and the whole, along with the western states of the Union organized into one empire, headed by a man of the enterprise and talents of Colonel Burr, will present a phenomenon in the political history of the globe perhaps only equaled by the Modern Empire of France." It appeared the entire Western Hemisphere was up for grabs. Walter McCaleb notes, "A paragraph of more startling political significance, so far as the New World is concerned, has perhaps never appeared in print."[32] Indeed, the Burr affair was a sticky matter, and critics suggested that Jefferson had taken part in it.

For months Jefferson had been receiving reports of Burr's plans from a variety of sources, but had ignored the issue. He had been warned that Wilkinson was in on the plot too, but did nothing regarding the general. His reasons for pretending innocence about the pending revolt are unknown. Burr's biographer, Buckner Melton, explains that "the Burr Conspiracy is full of mysteries, but this is one of the biggest," adding that "Jefferson's behavior was to grow still more bizarre."[33] When Jefferson proclaimed Burr in violation of the Proclamation of Neutrality (which President Washington had adopted years before to stifle Jefferson's own political activities), militias were alerted to capture Burr. He was stopped in Mississippi as he and an entourage of about a hundred men and women floated downriver on flatboats to begin the insurrection at New Orleans.

Burr was subjected to a series of grand jury trials as prosecutors, driven by Jefferson, tried to pin him down for treason or at least for violating the Neutrality Act. In Kentucky, Mississippi, and finally Virginia, Burr was tried again and again as Jefferson continued pushing for conviction. After a month-long trial in Richmond in August 1807, which riveted the nation's attention, a jury again found him not guilty of treason. Part of Burr's defense had been to incriminate Wilkinson and Jefferson, but adequate records could not be produced. As the legal historian Buckner Melton explains, "the trial of the century," quickly wound down and interest faded. Burr, broken and friendless, went to Europe.

Burr was fortunate—Wilkinson had enlisted several "bounty hunters," among them a half-dozen army members under his command, to capture and assassinate Burr before the Richmond trial even began. Among them was Moses Hooke, now a captain under Wilkinson, who had a few years earlier been selected by Meriwether Lewis as an alternate leader if William Clark had declined the trip west.

Meriwether Lewis attended the Richmond trial, Burr's last.

He sent almost daily reports to Thomas Jefferson, who remained at Monticello. After the verdict was read, Lewis embarked for his post in St. Louis, where he would take up his duties as governor of Louisiana. His brother, Reuben Lewis, accompanied him.

Burr escaped to exile after four trials and four acquittals. He arrived in England on June 9, 1808, where he tried to enlist the British government in a renewed scheme for conquest of the Spanish colonies in America. That failed, and so did an attempt to interest France along the same lines. When he tried to return home, Burr was denied a U.S. passport, the result of Jefferson's unrelenting harassment. McCaleb claims that the harassment of Burr, scorned as a criminal and mercilessly hounded by Jefferson, "constitutes the most sinister blotch in the escutcheon of Jefferson."[34] Eventually Burr returned to the United States. Destitute and alone, he set up a small law practice and married an older widow. The marriage failed, and so did his health. When news of the Texas revolution reached his boardinghouse, he exclaimed, "There! You see? I was right! I was only thirty years too soon. What was treason in me thirty years ago, is patriotism now!" He died alone in 1836. After a funeral ceremony at Princeton, he was buried there alongside his father and grandfather.[35]

Wilkinson not only exposed Burr's plot to Jefferson, he alerted Mexican Viceroy Iturrigaray in Mexico City as well, warning of a naval attack by insurgents on Vera Cruz. He asked the Spanish to reward him for the information in two installments of $85,000 and $36,000. But Iturrigaray had gained no new knowledge about Burr's intentions: "In my answer to the General I gave him to understand that the revolutionists had not caused me any alarm; for I had been long prepared to repel them by force, even though their numbers had been much greater."

Iturrigaray refused to pay, claiming he had no orders from the King.[36]

From today's vantage point, many scholars believe that Burr was not a separatist, that instead he sought to bring territories into the United States, such as an independent Florida or Texas. Certainly success at such a venture would have restored his political viability, would have redeemed him for the transgression of killing Alexander Hamilton, and would have given him as much luster as Jefferson gained from the Louisiana Purchase.

Henry Adams, great-grandson of John Adams, acknowledged that the key to understanding the relationship between Jefferson and Burr was Jefferson's relationship with Gen. James Wilkinson. At the time Adams wrote, other historians were unsure of Wilkinson's status as a Spanish agent. The evidence of Wilkinson's treason and of Burr's innocence was discovered by two graduate students, Walter Flavius McCaleb and Isaac Joslin Cox, who bicycled fifteen hundred miles across Mexico (dodging the action during the Mexican Revolution) to search dusty archives. They put the pieces together showing Wilkinson's role, and their findings reveal why Jefferson had to get rid of Burr.[37] Thomas Fleming writes of Wilkinson, "This disillusioned cash-hungry soldier did not have a moral bone in his body."[38] Wilkinson had a reputation for ambushes and assassinations; George Washington eventually referred to him as "that vile assassin."[39] Following the publication of conspiracy articles by the *World* newspaper in 1807, other papers across the nation devoured the story of treason and intrigue that implicated Burr along with General Wilkinson and leading politicians. "Many wonder how Wilkinson came to be appointed to the chief command of our forces," the *National Intelligencer* asked.[40]

Yet Jefferson gave full support to Wilkinson while continuing adamantly against Burr. "When Jefferson addressed Wilkinson personally, his loyalty was absolute," writes Donald Jackson. "To Wilkinson personally he was affable to the end."[41] Jackson confesses, "Giving Wilkinson the benefit of the doubt in the puzzling Burr affair, and conceding that Jefferson could not know that positive proof would eventually confirm Wilkinson's Spanish dealings, it is still difficult to comprehend his continued loyalty to the general."[42] Jefferson himself was a filibuster by stealth, supporting such efforts as early as 1796 for Genet, Michaux, and George Rogers Clark, all before he won the presidency. His opposition came from George Washington, who insisted the United States would not invade and plunder peaceful neighboring nations. Washington's proclamation to that effect was passed in Congress in 1794 as the Neutrality Act. It limited Jefferson's activities, but ironically it later became the act under which Jefferson prosecuted Burr for his filibuster efforts.[43] True, filibustering was only a misdemeanor under the act, but armed secession was treason, and it carried a death sentence. Jefferson sought that end for Burr, charging him with trying to divide the nation. Yet in 1804 he had casually written to Priestly that "whether we remain in one confederacy, or form into Atlantic and Mississippi confederacies, I believe not very important to the happiness of either part."[44] Jefferson's role in the Burr Conspiracy and his later persecution of Burr, as well as his support for Wilkinson, remain a puzzle.

THE SPANISH RESPONSE to Burr was clear and direct, just as it had been for the Lewis and Clark expedition. Spain placed more than a thousand men on the northern frontier to repel what they believed to be Jefferson's filibusters, turning back or capturing them all except for Lewis and Clark, who escaped because the forces and the Indians engaged to capture them had missed locating them.

When Lewis and Clark reached the Pacific, they claimed everything they traversed as U.S. territory, and for a while that went unchallenged. But in the Missouri watershed only the north bank was part of the Louisiana Purchase. The south bank remained Spanish, and indeed they continued to claim it. As Roger Kennedy points out, every time Lewis and Clark turned left from the river's bank, they were stepping on Spanish soil.[45]

9

Whatever Happened to Meriwether Lewis?

Nashville, Tennessee
18th Octr. 1809

Thos. Jefferson
Monticello, Virginia

Sir,
It is with extreme pain that I have to inform you of the death of His Excellency, Meriwether Lewis, Governor of upper Louisiana who died on the morning of the 11th Instant and I am sorry to say by suicide.
James Neely, U.S. agent to the Chickasaw Nation[1]

WHEN Lewis and Clark returned from their cross-continent trek, both had excellent political prospects. Neither faced a future in obscurity. Clark, however, had never been politically active, and he had his brother's reputation to overcome. He married his longtime sweetheart and settled down as an Indian agent and successful businessman in St. Louis, living to be sixty-eight years old. Lewis, however, was found dead only three years after the Corps of Discovery returned. He was buried haphazardly under a pile of rubble in Tennessee, termed a suicide, and forgotten.

The Pulitzer Prize–winning author David Leon Chandler, highly suspicious of Thomas Jefferson, noted that for twenty-five years after the winning of Independence, "those men who came of age in the Revolution—Hamilton, Burr, and Jefferson—would be at one another's throats and backs, locked in a fierce rivalry." Meriwether Lewis had been caught up in the intrigue surrounding the men and their machinations for taking control of the nation as well as its Western borders. Lewis "would become a victim to the ambition of all three men," according to Chandler. "But primarily to the schemes of his prince and mentor, Thomas Jefferson."[2]

After an early career as an exemplary soldier, as part of Jefferson's inner circle, and as a national hero, Meriwether Lewis was destined to become president one day. During the two years he lived in the president's house as Jefferson's private secretary, he was privy to events at the highest level of government. He could hold his own with frontiersmen as well as statesmen. He was a strong supporter of George Washington's philosophy of government and got along with the Federalists—in both, he was Jefferson's polar opposite. Too, Lewis was from Virginia, part of the dynasty of Virginia presidents that Jefferson envisioned running the country. Yet instead of priming Lewis for the 1808 presidential election, Jefferson shipped him off to St. Louis to fill the territorial governor's position there.

James Wilkinson had once held the post, and when Jefferson offered it to James Madison, he soundly rejected it. St. Louis was on the road to nowhere politically, and too distant to make travel to the East comfortable. It was still a hotbed of intrigue and corruption, as private trading companies and government policies created a cauldron of discontent. There were still hundreds of landless men who had hoped Burr would create opportunities for them. Disappointment was in the air in St. Louis at the same time investors vied for the tremendous financial opportunities in the fur trade. Indian discontent added to the complexity, as Jefferson's relocation policy pushed resentments and hostilities to the brink of disaster. And Spain remained a potential threat to stability.

AFTER A ROUND of receptions across the country and at the capital following his return from the expedition, Lewis needed a new career. Neither he nor Jefferson seemed to have made plans for what he would do once he returned from the Pacific. The Burr trials were heavy on Jefferson's mind too, as he was obsessed with both vengeance upon Burr and vindication of his own reputation. After Madison firmly refused the governor's post at St. Louis, Jefferson appointed Lewis to the position. On March 3, 1807, Congress gave Lewis and Clark each 1,600 acres of land, and each man who had gone on the expedition received 320 acres west of the Mississippi River.[3] The Senate approved Lewis's nomination as Louisiana's territorial governor the following week and assigned Clark to serve under Lewis as superintendent of Indian Affairs for Louisiana. After thirteen years in the army, Lewis resigned to take the position. Jefferson, after receiving a mandate in the 1804 landslide reelection, could give political patronage as he chose. Yet the two explorers were shunted off to the frontier, in what appears to be an effort never to hear from them again.

Today we realize the significance of Lewis's achievement,

but in 1807 anti-Lewis sentiment, directed against Jefferson, peppered the newspapers. The *Monthly Anthology,* printed in Boston, included a mean-spirited attack on some of the celebratory articles being published about Lewis. Titled "On the Discoveries of Captain Lewis," and written by John Quincy Adams, but unsigned, it ridiculed Jefferson, the actual target. The article pointed out that Lewis never did find the things Jefferson told him to look for—mammoths, Welsh Indians, or a mountain of salt. Lewis, Adams wrote, brought back nothing previously unknown and merely accomplished the naming of some rivers. The article did probe into Jefferson's scandalous personal life ("let dusky Sally henceforth bear the name of Isabella"), sniping at Jefferson's relationship with his slave Sally Hemings and his failure to confront Spain.[4]

Louisiana had changed while Lewis was in the West. While he was gone, American immigrants flooded in to what became a speculative frontier. "Violence, deceit, and character assassination became the guidelines of sociopolitical activity with, as always, basic economic motives lying at the bottom of every scrape," notes Richard Dillon, Lewis's biographer.[5] Jealousy was on all sides, even within the governor's office in St. Louis. After accepting Jefferson's official appointment to the post, Lewis remained in the East for months attending Burr's trial before heading west. In St. Louis, Frederick Bates officially took up the reins to act as governor until Lewis arrived.

Lewis had been a good friend of Frederick Bates's brother, Tarleton, and their connections went back years. In 1801 the Bates boys' father had had his heart set on one of them being selected as Thomas Jefferson's personal secretary. When he wrote to Frederick to tell him that Lewis had received the appointment, he confessed that "my golden dreams have been delusive!"[6] Rid-

dled with a long-held jealousy, the appointment of Frederick
Bates as Meriwether Lewis's stand-in as governor was fated for
disaster.

During his months in the East, Lewis discussed the printing
of his trip journals with printers, hired an illustrator to work on
the project, and worried about how to cover the estimated $4,500
cost of publication. Like everyone else, he also watched events
unfold in the repeated Burr trials. Because he spent a year in
Washington, attempting to govern Louisiana from a distance,
one might wonder if he ever really wanted the job. Meanwhile, in
the West, Bates was growing more comfortable with the position.
"His pride and jealousy soon festered into hatred," Richard Dillon explains. Bates wrote to Lewis that "contrary to my first expectations, you must expect to have some enemies." Certainly
Bates would be among them.[7]

Once Lewis arrived in St. Louis to take up the position, he
set Bates straight. He recognized that Bates's hostility promised
to create problems, and he confronted him about his attitude.
Bates insisted that while the two men had different ideas about
government, it was nothing personal. Lewis told him if that was
the case, he should avoid disagreeing with him in public. "When
we meet in public, let us at least, address each other with cordial-
ity," Lewis advised. Nevertheless Bates soon resumed undermin-
ing Lewis in order to gain personal popularity. Dillon calls Bates
a "pious fraud" who was clearly out to destroy Lewis.[8]

Along with being a very active governor, Lewis, like Clark,
sponsored a mixed-blood fur trader's child, the thirteen-year-old
son of René Jusseaumme, whom he brought to St. Louis for an
education. Lewis also financed a publisher in order to establish
the town's newspaper, the *Missouri Gazette*, for which he wrote
occasional articles under a pseudonym. He worked tirelessly on

Indian affairs, organizing the Indian Territory himself by restricting whites from entering areas reserved to the tribes. He prohibited whites from settling or farming on land that had Indian title. This policy made him extremely unpopular with some factions in St. Louis and the rest of Louisiana, and eventually in Washington.[9]

In an article about Indian policy for the *Missouri Gazette*, under the pen name "Clatsop," Lewis criticized both the Spanish and American policies toward Indians, especially the selling of traders' licenses and the practice of extending credit to Indians. He noted that whites sought to undermine one another in trade with the Indians, resulting in a lack of respect from them. The Sioux and Kansas tribes scorned whites, who would accept any deprecatory treatment from the Indians in order to continue trading, "The white men are like dogs; the more you beat and plunder them, the more goods they will bring you and the cheaper they will sell them," one Indian leader explained.[10] Lewis recognized that the situation was headed for violence. He viewed the government's Indian trade policy as a failure, believing that paying Indians to cooperate was not in the government's best interest. Bribing recalcitrant Indians with goods only fostered war and conflict, particularly between tribes.[11]

The U.S. army presented problems for Lewis too. The army was busy moving Indians to the West under Jefferson's relocation policy. Capt. George Armistead told Lewis he had no authority to interfere with the movement of Indians from their lands and that he would not recognize Cherokee land titles. As far as Armistead was concerned, whites could settle where they pleased. He challenged Lewis to prevent it and boasted he would obey no order given him by the governor.[12] Facing an uncooperative military, Lewis could scarcely rely on the militia, many of whom were busy running contraband to Mexico or trading illegally with the Indians. Horse thieves, murderers, cast-offs, and renegades seemed drawn to the St. Louis area, and Lewis must have been frustrated trying to deal with his constituency.

While American traders had lavished goods on the Missouri tribes in attempts to wind their favor from Spain and Britain, that policy had only created problems. Tribes rivaled one another for more goods and realized that American largesse increased according to Indian depredations. Lewis advocated restricting trade goods from Indians as a punishment, rather than resorting to violence to contain them when presents no longer worked. His view called for the government to restrict traders too, however. He advocated a line of government-regulated trade posts along the rivers to control the rampant fur, alcohol, and weapons trade. He pointed out that tribes who attacked traders could be cut off from trade goods, which would cause them to "make any sacrifice to regain the privilege they had previously enjoyed." Because the government had no resources to protect traders or settlers at that point, Lewis believed his idea would minimize frontier conflicts. "Their thirst of merchandise is paramount to every other consideration," he pointed out. "The leading individuals among them, well knowing this trait in the character of their own people, will not venture to encourage or excite aggressions on the whites when they know they are, themselves, to become the victims of its consequences."[13]

Opposition to Lewis's policies filtered east as well. Nicholas Boilvin, longtime Indian trader and a U.S. spy within the British fur trade, wrote to President Madison in 1809 in support of Lewis's Indian policy. Rumors had been rampant in St. Louis that Washington politicians were unhappy with Lewis, and Boilvin wanted to bolster support for Lewis in the nation's capital.

"Should Governor Lewis leave this quarter, I fear from what I hear among the Indians all would not be quiet long. They would be dissatisfied at the departure of their Father Lewis, as they style him. . . ." Yet the Indians were growing hostile to the increasing number of traders heading upstream. Fearing war between Spain and the United States was imminent, Lewis realized that the Indians—the Kansas, Great Pawnees, Loups, Omahas, Poncas, and the Pawnee Republic—remained allied with Spain, whereas the United States had less support. The Little Osages, Missouris, and part of the Great Pawnees, in all about a thousand men at most, alone favored the United States.[14]

In spite of Lewis's criticisms of government policy, he was not opposed to trade with the Indians. Historians speculate that he was likely a silent partner in the St. Louis Missouri Fur Company, formed by William Clark, Manuel Lisa, and Silvestre Labadie. Reuben Lewis, Meriwether's brother, was a stakeholder in the company, as well as an Indian agent under Clark. The company's mission was to wrest the lucrative upper Missouri River trade from the British, no easy task.[15]

Lewis had his hands full in St. Louis, yet he worked tirelessly at his job as well as being actively involved in the local social world. But one thing he did not do was to continue a correspondence with Thomas Jefferson. Some writers have suggested that Lewis was preoccupied with the governor's job and local political strife, but that seems unlikely.[16] He found time to write articles for the local newspaper, attend meetings at the Masonic lodge (which he founded), and more. Yet he never answered another letter from Thomas Jefferson. Jefferson complained bitterly that Lewis did not respond. Only a couple of coldly concise formal messages arrived from Governor Lewis.

In August 1809 Lewis began planning a trip to Washington

to meet with President Madison. Jefferson, now retired at Monticello, heard about it and wrote Lewis, attempting to reopen a dialogue. But Jefferson's letter did not reach St. Louis before Lewis departed. At the same time William Clark, his wife, and their infant son, Meriwether Lewis Clark, departed for Washington as well. Why the two men felt they needed to make the trip remains a mystery. Clark usually made an annual trip to visit relatives; Lewis did not. Yet they both set out at the same time. More mysteriously, they took different routes.

Lewis planned to go by ship out of New Orleans, and left on September 4 with his valet, John Pernier, accompanying him.[17] He took two trunks filled with papers, including his trip journals from the expedition, several rifles, pistols, tomahawks, and knives, along with a saddlebag he kept by his side, containing what he called "state papers."[18] After traveling downriver by barge for a few days, Lewis became ill, most likely with a continuing case of malaria. Lewis and Pernier went ashore at Fort Pickering, near Memphis, where they were guests of Maj. Gilbert Russell. Lewis had been stationed at Fort Pickering in 1797 but was not acquainted with Major Russell, who under Wilkinson's tutelage had just rejoined the army the year before, risen to major, and been given charge of the fort only four months earlier.

While resting at the fort, Lewis changed his mind about how he would proceed and decided to head overland. He explained that his change of course was due to fears of British attack at sea. The day after he arrived at Fort Pickering, Lewis sent a note to President Madison, informing him that he was heading inland through Mississippi and Tennessee to avoid "the original papers relative to my voyage to the Pacific falling into the hands of the British."[19] Eager to please, Russell offered to escort Lewis personally to Washington. Lewis waited for Wilkinson to give Russell permission to do so, but Wilkinson denied the request.

While many have ridiculed Lewis's concern with the British, even suggesting that Lewis was deranged, the longtime Lewis scholar Grace Miller points out that there was a widespread fear that British agents were spreading throughout the Southeast. Miller writes that "it is a matter of record that early in October, 1809, the Secretary of War had issued his directive warning against British agents infiltrating the Chickasaw country; and for a Company to be held in readiness to move South to the Fort at the Bluffs 'at a moment's notice.' "[20]

Lewis's health may have been a reason too. He admitted he was eager to get to a cooler climate because he was "very much exhausted from the heat. . . ." He may have feared his health would decline if he headed farther south, feverish as he was, and thus sought the cooler mountain air. Going overland rather than heading to humid New Orleans in September held more appeal to a man in the throes of malarial fever. Weak as he may have been, his letter to Madison is clear and lucid. He shows no hint of depression, writing that, "Provided my health permits, no time shall be lost in reaching Washington." He had duplicates of vouchers he planned to submit for payment when he arrived.[21] He was a man on a business trip with several planned meetings, objectives, and an unwavering sense of duty.

Major Russell at Fort Pickering played a significant role, according to writer David Leon Chandler, who points out that Russell was a Wilkinson protégé and one of the first to claim that Lewis was suicidal. Chandler notes that Russell lent Lewis a hundred dollars, two horses, and saddles, taking a promissory note from Lewis—the last note he ever wrote—as security. If indeed

Russell worried that Lewis was insane, as he later wrote, it is not likely he would have lent him the equivalent of four months of his army pay.

There was yet another player in the mystery, the federal Indian agent to the Chickasaws, James Neelly. Neelly had been appointed to his Chickasaw Bluffs post just six weeks before Lewis arrived—nominated to the post by James Wilkinson. Wilkinson was now stationed in New Orleans—a place Lewis was apparently suddenly wary of passing through.

When Wilkinson refused to allow Major Russell to accompany Lewis, it seemed serendipitous that James Neelly arrived shortly afterward, offering to accompany Lewis on his way through Chickasaw lands and along the Natchez Trace to Nashville. A few days out (they moved fifty miles a day, on horseback), they discovered two of the horses missing one morning, so Neelly went to round them up. He told Lewis and the two servants who accompanied them to go on ahead and wait for him at a settler's home and way station known as Grinder's stand, fifty miles north.

Ten days later the Nashville newspaper *Democratic Clarion* reported Lewis's death in a black-bordered obituary on page three. Lewis had arrived at the Grinder's place, where he and the servants obtained lodging for the night. Around midnight, Mrs. Grinder heard two pistol shots. The next morning the two servants looked in on the governor, who told them he had shot himself and begged for a drink of water. He lay down on the floor and died. A ball had grazed the top of his head and another had gone through his intestines. He reportedly slashed his neck, arm, and throat with a razor. He muttered something about a trunk of papers "that he said would be a great value to our government," the *Clarion* reported. "He had been under the influence of a deranging malady for about six weeks—the cause of which is unknown," the story explained.[22] The eulogy ended with a highly positive comment about Lewis's work in the territory, including his fair treatment toward Indians and his commitment to justice.

The news of Lewis's death spread quickly, and within a few weeks major papers carried the shocking story. Neelly was probably the source for the *Clarion* article, though no one is certain. He did write a letter describing the events to Jefferson two days before the newspaper article appeared, but that letter did not reach Jefferson for six weeks.

Neelly's letter to Jefferson has been studied intensely for almost two centuries. Upon it rests the explanation of Lewis's death as a suicide. Neelly wrote: "It is with extreme pain that I have to inform you of the death of His Excellency Meriwether Lewis, Governor of Upper Louisiana who died on the morning of the 11th Instant and I am sorry to say by Suicide." Neelly went on to explain how the two had traveled together, then split up to meet again at Grinder's. He wrote that "on our arrival at the Chickasaw nation I discovered that he appeared at times deranged in mind." When Mrs. Grinder discovered that Lewis was "deranged," Neelly related, she chose to sleep in a different house. He explained that the servants had heard gun shots at three in the morning and found Lewis "had shot himself in the head with one pistol & a little below the Breast with the other." Lewis had asked Pernier to get him water but had died shortly after.

Neelly had appeared on the scene later—"I came up some time after, & had him as decently Buried as I could in that place." He gathered Lewis's possessions and shipped everything to Jefferson. He noted that "some days previous to the Governor's death he requested of me in case any accident happened to him, to send his trunks with the papers therein to the President, but I think it very probable he meant to you."[23]

In one of those odd quirks of history, Thomas Freeman was given the task of carrying Lewis's belongings to Monticello. Freeman, a surveyor, had been part of the failed "scientific expedition" that Jefferson and Wilkinson had sent up the Red River in 1806, which had been stopped by the Spanish army. The expedition was largely kept secret, and references to its purpose were expunged from the few records that remain.[24] When that mission failed, Freeman was appointed as a government surveyor of land boundaries for the Chickasaw Treaty. Both Jefferson and Albert Gallatin (secretary of the treasury) had been pleased with his efforts there to maintain squatters' rights.[25] For some reason—either Wilkinson or serendipity—Freeman arrived just in time to personally carry Lewis's trunks and journals to Jefferson at Monticello. The official memorandum listing Lewis's possessions, dated November 23, 1809, states that the two trunks were "taken charge of by Thomas Freeman to be safe conveyed to Washington City."[26]

Freeman delivered the trunk of papers to Jefferson, however, instead of to President Madison. If there was anything in those trunks that might have reflected negatively on Jefferson and his legacy, we can assume he removed and destroyed the evidence. Lewis was on his way to a very important meeting with President Madison, yet we cannot be sure what he intended to discuss or present to the president. Only two years later, in 1811, James Wilkinson was brought to court over suspected complicity with Burr, and Wilkinson asked Freeman to testify in his favor, which Freeman eagerly did. Freeman also attempted to smear the character of a witness for the prosecution, claiming the elderly witness had invited Freeman to have sexual relations with himself and his washerwoman.[27]

John Pernier, Lewis's manservant, has remained an elusive figure in history. David Leon Chandler wrote, "Pernier has been variously described as a French Creole, a Spaniard, a mulatto, and a former servant of Jefferson's who had accompanied Lewis to St. Louis. . . ."[28] We do know that he arrived at Monticello on November 22, astride Lewis's horse, which Jefferson then gave to him. He stayed at Monticello four days before Jefferson dispatched him to take Lewis's effects and papers on to President Madison, to be distributed to Lewis's family.

In spite of Lewis's high profile and the mysterious circumstances surrounding his death, there was no official investigation. Jefferson took the lead in pointing out that Lewis's family had a strain of mental illness (which no historian has ever been able to find) and that Lewis was an alcoholic as well. How odd it seems that a man who spent years searching for elusive mammoth bones and Indian vocabularies in order to ferret out truth and meaning would skim over Lewis's demise so easily. Jefferson asked no questions, began no investigation. Talk about Lewis's death was hushed by calling it a suicide, which prevented anyone from digging further into the whole episode. Jefferson reinforced the suicide verdict in the preface he wrote to the Lewis and Clark expedition's journals, which were published by Paul Allen in 1814.[29]

The story remained closed there for nearly a century, until Elliott Coues published an edited edition of the journals in 1893, challenging the suicide theory.[30] He noted that in Tennessee, folks had called it murder. Oral history said that Lewis was shot from behind and discovered lying in a ditch by a mail rider passing over the trail. Local history also told of a coroner's jury making an inquest into Lewis's death, but that report has never been found.[31] The Tennessee legislature considered the issue in 1849 when it placed a monument over Lewis's grave.[32] "Mrs. Grinder told her story in at least three different versions, Captain Russell made two differing reports; a Negro servant and a white girl, materialized to claim having been at Grinder's that dreadful night," Richard Dillon writes. "Soon Lewis was said to have not only been shot in the forehead and side, but in the mouth, under the chin, and in the intestines."[33] In many stories, his throat was slashed as well as his arms. A grisly death, it grew even more so every time it was retold.

John Pernier, who might have been a witness to events, was silent. Thomas Jefferson wrote to a Lewis relative, William Meriwether, the year after Lewis's death, with the news that Pernier had "lately followed his master's example," reputedly killing himself in Washington.[34] His landlord was said to have described a broke and depressed Pernier, who took his life April 29, 1810, with laudanum.[35] Speculation about whether Pernier was murdered to seal his lips has never been proven. It simply became another of the many suspicious deaths attributed to suicide surrounding these events.

ALTHOUGH MANY HISTORIANS have accepted suicide as an explanation for Lewis's death, based on Thomas Jefferson's explanation, there are so many contradictions surrounding the event that a body of "murder" theorists has emerged. The Idaho writer Vardis Fisher took up the investigation in his book *Suicide or Murder? The Strange Death of Governor Meriwether Lewis*, published in 1962, looking at who may have had the opportunity to kill Lewis. David Leon Chandler's *The Jefferson Conspiracies: A*

President's Role in the Assassination of Meriwether Lewis, published in 1994, examines who might have had a motive.

Was robbery the motive? Certainly that was the most likely cause at that place and time. Lewis had a hundred dollars with him, but his expensive watch, custom pistols, dirk, matchbox, and other valuables were untouched.[36] Neelly did not return all of Lewis's personal possessions; Lewis's half brother, John Marks, later obtained Lewis's rifle from Neelly. If he had been a robbery victim, surely his belongings would have been taken.[37]

Those who knew and worked with Lewis never mentioned alcoholism or suicidal tendencies. No clue exists in the voluminous expedition diaries, either. William Clark, who knew him better than anyone, years later insisted that Lewis had not taken his own life.[38] Frederick Bates, Lewis's nemesis in the governor's office, would have eagerly pointed out Lewis's drinking or drug problem if he knew of it, as he looked for any way to undermine his superior. Yet he never mentioned alcoholism, drug abuse, or depression.[39] "Sensitive he was; neurotic he was not," biographer Richard Dillon explains. "Lewis was one of the most positive personalities in American history."[40] Assertions that he was despondent over his financial failures makes little sense; he had owned considerable landholdings since before the expedition, and was selling land to maintain his creditability. Lewis's financial problems were not a significant cause for suicide.

Reimert Ravenholt, a Seattle-area physician and epidemiologist, offers a unique explanation, pointing to Lewis's act as arising from insanity induced by a long-running case of syphilis. He insists the evidence that Lewis killed himself is "incontrovertible" and points out that Lewis did the deed to spare embarrassment to family and friends and prevent the possible tarnishing of the Corps of Discovery in case anyone realized his degenerative condition. Proponents of the suicide theory are left to battle whether it was due to syphilitic insanity or an insurmountable, recurring depression. Dr. Ravenholt argues that Stephen Ambrose's acceptance of psychological depression "impugns his [Lewis's] courage." Ravenholt adds that epidemiologists at the Centers for Disease Control believe neurosyphilis to be the cause of Lewis's suicide.[41]

More recently, investigations into Lewis's death have proposed to end the speculation by using scientific technology, such as forensic archaeology and DNA testing. But no one is certain that the body buried in the Tennessee grave is actually Meriwether Lewis. There were no witnesses to the death or the burial. The remains were later reburied when a monument was built by the state, but there was no way to prove they were actually Lewis's.

Most government and academic historians have held the line with Jefferson: it was suicide. No further digging necessary—the unfortunate man simply did himself in. The alternate explanation, however, probes at the government—particularly Jefferson, his cabinet, and the national expansionist policy that continued through Andrew Jackson's presidency. To question the suicide explanation would necessitate finding a perpetrator. Best to leave those dogs sleep, seems the response of many. Few scholars have dug into the Aaron Burr controversy, and few have seriously criticized Jefferson, other than his ugly exploitation of his own slaves. History buffs, reenactors, and amateur historians who have spent years studying the events and individuals usually maintain that Lewis's death was murder. In his best-selling book *Undaunted Courage*, Stephen Ambrose promoted the suicide theory to his wide reading audience. The hegemony of Ambrose's work will likely align most opinions with his. Ken Burns, a popular documentary filmmaker, also endorsed the suicide theory in his film about Lewis and Clark.

In May 1996 a coroner's jury listened as Professor James Starrs of Georgetown Law School, along with a team of historians, pathologists, psychiatrists, and firearms experts, reexamined events surrounding Lewis's mysterious death. The jury watched as experts fired replica muzzle-loading pistols just like Lewis's handguns, examined Lewis's handwriting samples, and ultimately recommended the exhumation of Lewis's remains.

Starrs, a forensic specialist, requested permission to exhume Lewis's purported remains from the National Park Service, which owns and controls the ground around the burial site in Tennessee. The Park Service refused, which led to a public hearing in December 1997. Starrs testified with the help of Lewis's nearest living relative, Dr. William Anderson, a great-great-grandson of Lewis's sister. One hundred sixty Lewis descendants joined in the request. Anderson spoke for the descendants, explaining, "It's been especially distressful as the bicentennial approaches as there has been a tendency to picture him [Lewis] as a bumbling, drunken incompetent—syphilitic by some accounts—who couldn't even commit suicide properly." The family wants to learn whatever the remains might reveal, and they want a Christian reburial—which was never done.[42]

The debate moved from obscure history journals to national attention when the Park Service resisted Starr's efforts, claiming it might set a precedent for further exhumations on Park Service grounds. Opposition came from historians as well. Stephen Ambrose dismissed the murder theory and assailed Starr's efforts, even admonishing President Clinton to step in and stop the proposed exhumation.

Starrs believes that historians resisted his project because he

SEDUCED BY THE WEST

was a scientist—an interloper on their turf. "I tend to side with Voltaire," he explained. "Voltaire said that God in all of his omnipotence can't change the past. That's why he created historians."[43] He points out that by preventing a scientific inquiry, possible today with improved technology, we are only relying on circumstantial evidence. According to Starrs, the explanation might as well include one local resident's speculation that Robert Grinder came home, found Lewis in bed with his wife, and shot him.[44]

Richard Williams, manager of the Lewis and Clark National Historic Trail for the National Park Service, may have the most pragmatic view. "It may be better that it is a mystery," Williams notes. "That way people can choose what to believe."[45] That does not mean the Lewis and Clark saga should be approached as a sort of "choose your own adventure" tale. Without a "happy ending," the Lewis and Clark story seems to endure, the mystery behind Lewis's death resulting in much more research and dialogue than if the cause of Lewis's death were certain. That mystique, the unresolved conclusion, may be what keeps us wondering and digging into the events and people surrounding him.

The monument erected over Lewis's grave in 1848, near Hohenwald, Tennessee, declares: "Of courage undaunted, possessing a firmness and perseverance of purpose which nothing but impossibilities could divert from its direction." Richard Dillon sums it up: "What more fitting, if belated, epitaph could we compose for the man who opened up and secured the Far West to the United States at such small cost, a mere $38,722.25 (according to War Department accountant Simmons)—and Lewis's life."[46]

So for now we suppose that Meriwether Lewis lies undisturbed in rural Tennessee. Perhaps someday he will be given what many others believe is his due—burial at Arlington National Cemetery.

10

The Wrest
of the West

*Every moment of your grandfather's society that I lose, is
irreparable.—Nicholas Trist to Thomas Jefferson's
granddaughter, Virginia Randolph, 1822*[1]

THE BRITISH were not idle bystanders when it came to
westward expansion. One of their own tried to beat Lewis
and Clark to the mouth of the Columbia River, but was not quick
enough. In 1807 David Thompson, a British-born orphan who
had been recruited into the Canadian fur trade, set out from the
Canadian interior, heading overland across the Rockies to the
Pacific coast. He and his group hoped to stake a claim for his em-
ployer, the North West Company, if not for Britain. With eight
men, a canoe, and twenty-three horses, he traveled from the
Canadian Rockies to the Columbia River. In present-day northern Idaho he stopped with the Kootenai Indians, who told him a
party of Americans had passed through farther south about three

weeks earlier, which would have been the last week of July 1807. The Indians reported that a group of forty-two men had built a military post at the confluence of the Snake and Columbia rivers. Two of the Americans had accompanied Lewis and Clark, the Indians claimed. "This establishment of the Americans will give a new Turn to our so long delayed settling of this Country, on which we have entered it seems too late," Thompson lamented.[2]

The mysterious Americans promptly sent him a letter warning Thompson to stay out of the region, that it was now under U.S. control. The letter, carried by Indian courier, was signed July 10, 1807, and listed the address as "Fort Lewis, Yellow River, Columbia." The order was issued in the name of Captain Jeremy Pinch. Yet no historical records in the United States or Canada list such a person. The name, an alias, provoked speculation by historians for years, particularly after it surfaced in obscure documents in the public records in London. Did the United States send another military unit upriver following the Lewis and Clark party? If a party had reached the upper Columbia by mid-1807, it would have met Lewis and Clark as they were returning downriver, reaching St. Louis in September 1806. Yet there is no mention in the expedition journals about a U.S. military party, nor a record in St. Louis of such an outfit setting off upriver. The mysterious Fort Lewis, and Lieutenant Pinch (sometimes referred to as Zachary Perch, because the handwriting is hard to read), have taunted historians for decades.

David Thompson made no response to the warning letter, which listed several regulations that he must adhere to in this new American territory: no liquor sales to Indians; no flags to be flown except that of the United States; no medals to be given to the Indians; no goods traded at above a fixed price; no acts of revenge or punishment against the Indians; and a customs duty to be paid on all goods. That duty was not to be paid in cash but in "kind," meaning in furs, in the field.[3] The payment of furs in the field meant that when the Canadians encountered U.S. "customs agents," they had to surrender furs on the spot, negating a paper trail and currency which could be traced. Was this an attempt to set up a legitimate trading post? More likely it was a party of renegades positioning themselves in the mountains, posturing and blustering in the wake of Lewis and Clark's successful venture, and pocketing the profits. Who were they, and who equipped them?

Jeremy Pinch wrote a second letter, calling his location Poltito Palton Lake, and referring to the chief of the "Poltito palton."[4] Thompson figured they were the Green Wood Indians and were fighting with the "Fall Indians." In the second letter, Pinch addressed Thompson as "the British Merchant Trafficking with the Kootenaes" and warned him sternly that by not responding to Pinch's first missive, he had taken the offensive. "Your silence Sir I am to construe into a tacit disrespect, and thereby am apt to think you do not acknowledge the authority of Congress over these Countries, which are certainly the property of the United States both by discovery and Cession." If such was the case, Pinch warned that "you must learn Sir that we have more powerful means of persuasion in our hands than we have hitherto used, we shall with regret apply Force, but where necessary it will be done with vigor, so as fully to enforce the Decrees of Congress." He added a threat, "If my private opinion be of any weight, you nor any British Merchant will be suffered to traffic with our Indian Allies."[5]

Whoever Pinch was, it was clear the letters were a bluff. Military protocol would never have added such bluster as this: "As soon as our Military Posts are fortified, strong Patroles will be sent out to survey the Country and where necessary and eligible American Merchants will be placed who will second the philanthropic views of Congress in the Civilization of the Natives. You will see the necessity of submitting and with a good grace. . . ." Pinch predicted it would be but a short time until the region was governed as closely as "New York or Washington."[6]

Who were the mysterious Americans? The historian Alvin Josephy writes that "who had sent them, where they had located their military post, or what eventually happened to them are all mysteries." He notes that the Green Wood Indians were Nez Perce people, whom the British had not yet begun trading with.[7] He does suspect that an expedition sent out by General Wilkinson under direction of his longtime associate, artillery officer Capt. John McClallen, may have been involved. The language in Pinch's warning letters is remarkably similar to letters Zebulon Pike took with him, written under General Wilkinson in a sort of self-styled frontier boilerplate.[8] If Wilkinson was behind the effort to set up a private trading empire in the Pacific Northwest, the similarity in documents may point in that direction.

John McClallen and a company loaded with trade goods headed upriver and met Lewis and Clark as they were returning downriver in September 1806. Lewis and McClallen already knew each other, having served together in the army. Now, meeting in the wilds, the two shared gossip from home as well as delicacies McClallen had brought along, including a bottle of wine. McClallen filled the adventurers in on the news. "One rumor had them wiped out to a man, another had them prisoners of the Spaniards and laboring in the mines of New Spain," Richard Dillon explains.[9] After a convivial visit, the parties headed their separate ways.

The historian John C. Jackson believes that the mysterious

Jeremy Pinch was John McClallen, who had a long history of working closely with General Wilkinson. After meeting Lewis and Clark, McClallen spent the winter with the Yankton Dakota, and because of resistance from Spanish Pawnee allies, decided to head to New Mexico on the Yellowstone River. Jackson believes that it was McClallen who wrote the mysterious letter warning Canadian and British traders that the area was now controlled by the United States. Having no military authority at all (his venture was privately funded by Wilkinson), McClallen bluffed his way, signing with an alias. After passing the letter to Indian couriers, McClallen and his forty-plus party settled in the Bitterroot Valley, setting up camp near present-day Missoula, Montana.

McClallen's efforts stopped Thompson and the Canadians from moving aggressively into the Columbia River drainage. McClallen and his men returned to the Yellowstone River for the winter. The following spring they headed back into the mountains. David Thompson reported that Indians told him an American officer and eight men were killed by a war party in May 1808. Surely the mysterious American party was but one more of the independent efforts to attain control of the Pacific Northwest.

Another party left St. Louis in the summer of 1806, led by Manuel Lisa, the crafty, ambitious trader who had caused Meriwether Lewis such chagrin in 1803 as he was outfitting the expedition. Lisa took along about forty men and picked up John Colter and George Drouillard, both returning veterans of the Lewis and Clark expedition. The following year Lisa sent several trapping parties up the Missouri and tried to open up trade into Santa Fe. Lisa partnered with his former chief rival, Auguste Choteau, and the two formed the St. Louis Missouri Fur Company. Other partners included Benjamin Wilkinson (the general's brother), Reuben Lewis (Meriwether's brother), and William Clark, now the Indian agent for the Louisiana Territory. The band of merchants set out to exploit the newly opened fur markets but spent much of their energies protecting one another from their own dishonesty. The effort met with deserters, debts, theft, and lack of supplies, until upriver a band of Blackfeet attacked and killed eight men and burned the fur storehouse to the ground. Then Jefferson's Embargo Act killed the market in furs. Success was fleeting. When Manuel Lisa and Pierre Choteau returned from the mountains in November 1809, they learned that Meriwether Lewis was dead. As one observer put it, "The hopes of the Fur Company which ascended this River have died with their patron and benefactor *Governor Lewis.*"[10]

A myriad of eager, creative, and undaunted individuals sought to grab hold of the West, acquiring a foothold or a vast empire for themselves. From John Ledyard to Meriwether Lewis, there were also selfless men who sought simply to go there, to blaze a path for others to follow. Behind them there would always be a clutch of eager entrepreneurs and politicians seeking wealth and power. Whether they wished to overthrow a government or just make money, the West beckoned like nothing else had before, or would after. And in the early nineteenth century no one even realized that gold lay scattered across its vast expanses.

As a final act in this Western drama that shaped a nation and a continent, one more independent, lone-cannon individual brings the tale to a close. In 1848, about forty years after the Lewis and Clark expedition returned from the Pacific, an obscure State Department clerk, Nicholas Trist, negotiated what amounted to a private treaty with Mexican officials, ending the war with Mexico and sweeping more than half of Mexico's territory into the United States. Called the Treaty of Guadalupe Hidalgo, the terms of the agreement extended the nation's boundaries another half-million square miles, adding California, Nevada, Utah, most of New Mexico and Arizona, and swaths of Wyoming and Colorado to the United States, in exchange for $15 million in reparations for the Mexican War. Virtually single-handed, Trist shaped the agreement, doing what so many others had tried to do by assembling armies—wrest Spanish America from Hispanic control. Just as Burr, Wilkinson, and dozens of others from various nations had hoped to do, he took Mexico (or much of it), but without firing a shot.

How a government clerk found himself in such a situation makes an interesting story. Nicholas Trist has disappeared from American history, merely mentioned as a clerk who defied his superiors. But in an era of fascinating individuals who shaped the nation's history, he is worth further examination. Like Meriwether Lewis, he was Virginia-born (in Charlottesville, 1800). Thomas Jefferson appointed Nicholas Trist's father tax collector in Natchez in 1802, as a gesture of goodwill because while in Washington he often stayed at a boardinghouse run by Trist's grandmother. Trist's father died in 1804 when the boy was only four years old.

In 1817, long after he had left the presidency, Jefferson invited Mrs. Trist's two grandsons to visit his family at Monticello. Nicholas, then seventeen, and Jefferson, seventy-five, got along remarkably well. Jefferson nudged the boy into West Point Military Academy, where he considered leaving to join the Colombian military after hearing that cadets were starting there with a major's rank. After three years he dropped out and began courting Jefferson's granddaughter, Virginia Randolph, through letters to her parents. He took up the study of law, eventually moving back to Monticello to study under Jefferson. He married Virginia

Randolph and became her grandfather's private secretary.[11] Trist did pass the Virginia bar but took only one case to court.[12] He was more interested in modeling his life after Jefferson; he read widely, perfected his writing, and mastered foreign languages. When Lafayette visited Jefferson at Monticello in 1824, young Nicholas Trist was at his side. Two years later, when Jefferson was dying, Trist stood with family members at the bedside.

In 1828 Trist obtained a clerk's position in the State Department, precisely as a charitable gesture for his mother-in-law. Through connections he went on to become President Andrew Jackson's personal secretary. In 1833 Jackson sent Trist off to Havana, where he served as American consul to Cuba. The Caribbean cast a shadow over Trist's career; in 1839 Yankee ship captains filed two hundred charges against him, claiming he favored Spanish interests. Britain charged him with activity in the illegal slave trade between Africa and the Caribbean. A year later, when the presidential election shifted political patronage, he lost his position and returned to a clerk's job in the State Department.

In 1846 Jefferson's long-sought war with Mexico began—in a strikingly similar manner to how it might have begun in 1804. President James Polk had been elected on the promise of extending the nation's boundaries. Once a treaty with Britain delivered the Oregon country in early 1846, Mexico was next in line. A U.S. diplomat went to Mexico City offering $30 million for California and New Mexico, but was rebuffed. Polk lost his patience and wanted to attack Mexico, but a cabinet member suggested that the people would need more than the expulsion of a diplomat to get behind such an action. As during Jefferson's tenure, something larger was necessary to incite the public's wrath. When news arrived that Mexican forces had killed sixteen Americans near the Rio Grande, the stage was set. Polk quickly sent a war message to Congress, which voted overwhelmingly to commence what became known as "Mr. Polk's War."[13]

Trist was a lackluster, Spanish-speaking clerk who was an avid Democrat—exactly right for President Polk's plan. The United States was at war with Mexico, in an action neither nation felt very strongly about. Nevertheless Gen. Winfield Scott had taken troops into the port of Vera Cruz, then marched on the capital at Mexico City and now held it. But for what? Mexican military officials wavered and kept changing leadership, and the political climate was chaotic. No one wished to negotiate. Since Polk did not really want to end the debacle yet, hoping for more territory than what might be amenable to Mexico, he was in no rush to end the standoff either. Winfield Scott as military leader should have been the chief negotiator, but that would have made him victor of the war and the peace, and a prime candidate for the White House in 1848. Polk was pragmatic and patient, and thought someone like Trist, a faceless Democrat, a better choice to negotiate.[14]

Polk and many politicos, particularly Southern interests, hoped to annex *all* of Mexico. For expansionists it was the opportune time to push a bit harder, for more than the Southwest. Polk wanted it all, and he planned to enjoin Congress to demand larger land cessions as the price of peace "if Mexico protracted the war."[15]

In 1847 Trist was thus sent to Mexico to negotiate an end to the Mexican War, by a president who hoped he would drag his feet. Nevertheless Trist sat across the table from three Mexican officials and charmingly negotiated away more than half their country. To Polk, however, it was *not* good news. Consequently the president was furious when he learned of Trist's unauthorized activities, which by now also included a plan between Trist and General Scott to use some of Scott's war budget to bribe Mexican officials. Polk rushed a courier off with a letter recalling the diplomatic busybody. Trist ignored Polk's letter when it arrived, and wrote back that he intended to stay where he was and continue negotiating a peace settlement as a private citizen. Enraged, Polk called Trist "arrogant, impudent," and "destitute of honour or principle."[16] "He has acted worse than any man in the public employ I have never known," the president declared.[17]

With both Trist and Scott ignoring him, Polk could do nothing but fume. Five weeks later the treaty arrived, replete with the signatures and seals of three Mexican officials, and Nicholas Trist. The House of Representatives had opposed Polk's War; many Americans saw it as a move to gain additional territory that would strengthen slavery interests. Polk felt he had little support in Congress to continue funding a war in Mexico, and without funding he would essentially abandon the U.S. troops there. In addition, the upcoming election forced him to send Trist's treaty on to the Senate, where Southern interests led by Jefferson Davis sought to extend the boundaries farther into Mexico, reviving the war.

The Senate battled over the annexation, but since rejecting it would mean resuming an unpopular war, Trist's treaty was finally ratified by a vote of 38 to 14. Mexico accepted the terms, and the nation was blessed with extensive lands in the Southwest and California. "This gigantic step in the growth of the American republic was not taken with enthusiasm by either President or Congress," the historian David Potter notes. The lack of enthusiasm "resulted from the fact that the elements in opposition could find no viable alternative and no basis on which they could combine."[18] Almost in spite of itself, the nation had grown.

WHEN Thomas Jefferson died, he left more than $100,000 in debts, which his daughter and grandchildren were forced to pay. They sold some of Jefferson's slaves, leased others out, and began liquidating assets to pay debt. Jefferson's daughter Martha, Nicholas Trist's mother-in-law, relied on him to help arrange things, and he became administrator of the estate. The family could find no buyers interested in the family home at Monticello. The mansion, Jefferson's incredibly personal and eccentric trophy, held little appeal for anyone else. It may have been considered a misguided effort by a frivolous eccentric. But as the house sat, Trist was busy, sorting through all of Jefferson's personal papers. He acted as Jefferson's personal secretary in the years before his death, and now commenced sorting and filing the contents of Jefferson's six filing cabinets. In 1848 the family sold the lot of papers to Congress, where they are now held by the Library of Congress.

Trist, a self-motivated and perceptive individual, as well as a family member and protégé of Jefferson, would have undertaken to remove any documents from the collection that might cast a shadow on his mentor's legacy. We will never know what Trist may have removed from public view. There were no shredders in the 1830s, but there were adequate fireplaces.

Later that same year, 1848, Trist felt confident enough to write the treaty papers on his own in Guadalupe Hidalgo, a few miles north of Mexico City. He engineered a deal that Jefferson would have admired: gaining 55 percent of Mexico's territory for $15 million. And, like Robert Livingston who negotiated to buy Louisiana, he had done it ostensibly on his own, acting without advice or approval from the president. It was Trist who took up Jefferson's mantle—as lawyer, diplomat, and deal-maker. Meriwether Lewis, like John Ledyard, did not have the same sort of character or abilities. Lewis and Ledyard were fearless men who blazed the trail. Others, like Trist, would follow and do the paperwork.

The impact of the Lewis and Clark expedition did not end with their return to St. Louis, nor with Meriwether Lewis's untimely death. There was never an endeavor to equal it in U.S. history, except perhaps John Glenn's trip into space. The nation and the world altered their paradigm about the rest of the continent, which became solid ground now, and was not simply an abstraction, reached only by sea.

Notes

PREFACE

1. Donald Jackson, *Thomas Jefferson and the Stony Mountains: Exploring the West from Monticello* (Norman, Okla., 1993), p. xix.
2. Gerald S. Snyder, *In the Footsteps of Lewis and Clark* (Washington, D.C., 1970), p. 14.

CHAPTER 1. AWAY TO THE NORTH PACIFIC

1. A. P. Nasatir, *Before Lewis and Clark: Documents Illustrating the History of the Missouri, 1785–1804,* II (Lincoln, Nebr., 1990), 380.
2. Walter A. McDougall, *Let the Sea Make a Noise: Four Hundred Years of Cataclysm, Conquest, War and Folly in the North Pacific* (New York, 1993), p. 29.
3. Alexander DeConde, *This Affair of Louisiana* (New York, 1976), p. 8.
4. David J. Weber, *The Spanish Frontier in North America* (New Haven, Conn., 1992), p. 198.
5. Ibid., p. 197.
6. Roger G. Whitlam, "Conflict on the Periphery: Spanish Settlement on the Northwest Coast," *Columbia* (Summer 1992), p. 30.
7. Warren L. Cook, *Flood Tide of Empire: Spain and the Pacific Northwest, 1543–1819* (New Haven, Conn., 1973), p. 93.
8. Whitlam, p. 31.
9. Cook, p. 113.

10. Donald C. Cutter, "The Other Explorers: Alcalá Galiano and Valdés," *Columbia* (Summer 1991), p. 21; Cook, p. 319.
11. Jackson, *Jefferson*, p. 84.
12. Raymond H. Fisher, *Bering's Voyages: Whither and Why* (Seattle, 1977), p. 152.
13. Nasatir, pp. 495–499, for excerpts from Evans's journal.
14. Nasatir, pp. 410–414.
15. Ibid., p. 416.
16. David Williams, "John Evans' Strange Journey: Part II, Following the Trail," *American Historical Review*, vol. 54, no. 3 (April 1949), 528.
17. Jackson, *Jefferson*, p. 66.
18. Weber, p. 285.
19. Cook, p. 361.
20. McDougall, p. 91.
21. Weber, p. 272.
22. Ibid., p. 281.
23. Ibid., p. 274.
24. David Lavender, "Empires in the Northwest," *American Heritage*, August 1956, p. 83.
25. Ibid., p. 80.

CHAPTER 2. TO THE WEST BY EAST: JOHN LEDYARD'S VENTURE

1. Jared Sparks, *The Life of John Ledyard, the American Traveller; Comprising Selections from His Journals and Correspondence* (Cambridge, Mass., 1828), p. 172.
2. James Kenneth Munford, ed., *John Ledyard's Journal of Captain Cook's Last Voyage* (Corvallis, Ore., 1963), p. xxxiv.
3. Ibid., p. xxiii.
4. Ibid., p. ix.
5. Sparks, p. 82.
6. Ibid., p. 87.
7. Ibid., p. 90.
8. Munford, p. xlvi.
9. Stephen Watrous, ed., *John Ledyard's Journey Through Russia and Siberia, 1787–1788* (Madison, Wisc., 1966), p. 13.
10. Sparks, p. 161.
11. Munford, pp. 963, 8.

12. Ibid., p. xxxiii.
13. Sparks, p. 165.
14. Watrous, p. 95.
15. Sparks, p. 174.
16. Ibid., p. 174.
17. Ibid., p. 176.
18. Ibid., p. 177.
19. Jefferson to Ledyard, August 16, 1786, Jefferson Papers, Library of Congress.
20. Watrous, p. 128.
21. Ibid., p. 130.
22. Jackson, *Jefferson*, p. 50.
23. Watrous, pp. 258–259.
24. Sparks, p. 286.
25. Watrous, p. 31.
26. Ibid., p. 257.
27. Munford, p. 70.
28. Ibid., p. xliv.
29. Watrous, p. 38.
30. Sparks, p. 325.

CHAPTER 3. THE FRENCH BOTANIST, THE FADING WAR HERO, AND DREAMS OF EMPIRE

1. Harlow Giles Unger, *Noah Webster: The Life and Times of an American Patriot* (New York, 1998), p. 180.
2. Jefferson to George Rogers Clark, December 4, 1783, Jefferson Papers, Library of Congress.
3. It was common knowledge, says Donald Jackson, that Clark may have been already too unfit from alcoholism to make a Western trip. Jackson, p. 62.
4. Frederick Jackson Turner, "The Origin of Genet's Projected Attack on Louisiana and the Floridas," *American Historical Review*, vol. 3, no. 4 (July 1898), 652.
5. DeConde, p. 50.
6. John Carl Parish, "The Intrigues of Doctor James O'Fallon," *Mississippi Valley Historical Review*, vol. 17, no. 2 (September 1930), 236.
7. Turner, p. 652.

8. Parish, p. 241.
9. Ibid., p. 244.
10. Ibid., p. 248.
11. Ibid., p. 247.
12. Turner, p. 650.
13. Isaac Joslin Cox, "The Louisiana-Texas Frontier," *Quarterly of the Texas State Historical Association*, vol. X, no. 1 (July 1906), 46.
14. Unger, p. 179.
15. Ibid., p. 180.
16. Cox, p. 42.
17. Ibid., p. 181.
18. Ibid., p. 180.
19. Ibid., p. 181.
20. Ibid., p. 176.
21. Turner, p. 655.
22. Ibid.
23. Martin Sauer, *An Account of a Geographical and Astronomical Expedition to the Northern Parts of Russia . . . Performed by Commodore Joseph Billings, in the Years 1785 to 1794* (London, 1802), Appendix V, pp. 30–46. Sparks, p. 271.
24. DeConde, p. 79.
25. Jefferson to Madison, May 19, 1793, Jefferson Papers, Library of Congress.
26. Unger, p. 182.
27. Ibid., p. 183.
28. Turner, p. 665.
29. Unger, p. 181.
30. Turner, p. 666.
31. Unger, p. 188.
32. Ibid., p. 184.
33. Turner, p. 669.
34. Reuben Gold Thwaites, ed., *Journal of Andre Michaux, 1793–1796*, vol. III, *Early Western Travels, 1748–1846* (Cleveland, Ohio, 1904), p. 42.
35. Unger, p. 185.
36. Turner, p. 671.
37. George Rogers Clark, "George Rogers Clark to Genet, 1794," *American Historical Review*, vol. 18, no. 4 (July 1913), 782.
38. Parish, p. 252.

39. Ibid., p. 261.
40. Ibid., p. 262.

CHAPTER 4. WILD HORSES, YELLOW JOURNALISTS,
AND A LOVER OF GLORY

1. Noel M. Loomis, "Philip Nolan's Entry into Texas in 1800," in John
   Francis McDermott, ed., *The Spanish in the Mississippi Valley, 1762–1804*
   (Urbana, Ill., 1974), p. 132.
2. Jefferson to Nolan, June 24, 1798, Jefferson Papers, Library of Congress.
3. Cox, p. 56.
4. Jefferson to Dunbar, Jan. 16, 18—; http://lonestar.texas.net/~mdmclean/
   rc_papers_vol-1/019.htm
5. "F. A. Michaux's Travels West of Allegheny Mountains, 1802" in
   Thwaites, pp. 105, 306.
6. McDermott, p. 125.
7. Thwaites, p. 81.
8. Robert H. Thonhoff, book review, "Philip Nolan and Texas: Expeditions
   to the Unknown Land, 1791–1801, by Maurine T. Wilson and Jack Jackson," *Southwestern Historical Quarterly*, p. 124.
9. Winston De Ville and Jack Jackson, "Wilderness Apollo," *Southwestern
   Historical Quarterly*, vol. 92, no. 3 (1989), 454.
10. Loomis, p. 129.
11. Ibid., p. 132.
12. Cox, p. 59.
13. Loomis, p. 132.
14. Richard N. Rosenfeld, *American Aurora* (New York, 1997), p. 37.
15. Ibid., p. 43.
16. Ibid., p. 25.
17. Ibid., p. 39.
18. Ibid., p. 162.
19. Ibid., p. 215.
20. Ibid., p. 213.
21. Ibid., p. 96.
22. Ibid., p. 555.
23. Ibid., p. 671.
24. Ibid., p. 737.
25. Ibid., p. 799.

26. James Thomson Callender, *The Prospect Before Us*, vol. 2, part 2 (Richmond, Va., 1801), 96.

27. Ibid.

28. J. T. Callender, Richmond Recorder, October 20, 1802.

29. Joseph J. Ellis, *American Sphinx: The Character of Thomas Jefferson* (New York, 1998), p. 260.

30. Ibid., p. 211.

31. Ibid., p. 282.

32. William Safire, *Scandalmonger* (New York, 2000), p. 437.

33. Weber, p. 285.

34. Anthony F. C. Wallace, *Jefferson and the Indians: The Tragic Fate of the First Americans* (Cambridge, Mass., 1999), p. 15.

35. DeConde, p. 47.

36. Ibid., p. 62.

37. Richard Dillon, *Meriwether Lewis: A Biography* (Santa Cruz, Calif., 1988), p. 26.

38. Jackson, *Jefferson*, p. 121.

39. Dillon, p. 7.

40. Ibid., p. 9.

41. Ibid., p. 14.

42. Ibid., p. 25.

43. Jackson, *Jefferson*, p. 164.

44. Dillon, p. 34.

45. DeConde, p. 137.

46. Dillon, p. 30.

47. Ibid., p. 31.

48. Ibid., p. 38.

49. Donald Jackson, ed., *Letters of the Lewis and Clark Expedition with Related Documents, 1783–1854* (Urbana, Ill., 1962), p. 115.

50. Dillon, p. 91.

51. Ibid., p. 75.

52. Ibid., p. 31.

53. Jackson, *Jefferson*, p. 128.

54. Ibid., p. 129.

55. Dillon, p. 32.

56. Jackson, *Letters*, p. 23.

57. Ibid., p. 27.

58. Dillon, p. 49.

59. Jackson, *Letters*, p. 5.
60. Dillon, p. 75.
61. Ibid.
62. Ibid., p. 84.
63. Ibid., p. 76.
64. Ibid., p. 53.
65. DeConde, p. 68.
66. Ibid., p. 140.
67. Ibid., p. 201.
68. Ibid., p. 213.
69. Weber, p. 291.
70. DeConde, p. 178.
71. Ibid., p. 187.
72. Dillon, p. 79.

CHAPTER 5. PREPARATIONS

1. Nasatir, p. 728.
2. Dillon, p. 83.
3. DeConde, p. 218.
4. Ibid., p. 214.
5. Lewis to Clark, in Jackson, *Letters*, pp. 58–60. Original at Missouri Historical Society Library, St. Louis. Spelling here has been standardized; such was not the case in Lewis and Clark's time, making their writing appear unsophisticated and substandard. American spelling was not standardized until Noah Webster devised his spelling book, which was highly successful because it broke new ground. Writers had been spelling words in various ways; no spelling had been considered "inaccurate."
6. Ibid., pp. 61–66.
7. Ibid., p. 34.
8. Fisher, p. 127.
9. Ibid., p. 144.
10. Jackson, *Letters*, p. 35.
11. Ibid., p. 52.
12. Ibid., p. 100.
13. Ibid., p. 106.
14. Ibid., p. 137.
15. Ibid., p. 112.

16. DeConde, p. 219.
17. Ibid., p. 198.

Chapter 6. The Perfect Bait

1. Weber, p. 294.
2. Dillon, p. 82.
3. Jackson, *Letters*, p. 142.
4. Ibid., p. 155.
5. Cook, p. 453.
6. Ibid.
7. Jackson, *Letters*, p. 185.
8. Ibid.
9. Ibid., p. 173.
10. Ibid., p. 212.
11. Ibid., p. 188.
12. Ibid., p. 184.
13. Dillon, p. 97.
14. Ibid., p. 105.
15. Nasatir, p. 743. Cited in Weber, p. 294.
16. Dillon, p. 83.
17. Wallace, p. 228.
18. Cook, p. 460.
19. Ibid., p. 461.
20. Ibid., p. 462.
21. Ibid., p. 463.
22. Frank Bergon, ed., *The Journals of Lewis and Clark* (New York, 1989), p. 22.
23. Elliott Coues, ed., *The History of the Lewis and Clark Expedition by Meriwether Lewis and William Clark*, 3 vols. (New York, 1979), I, 69.
24. Dillon, p. 86.
25. DeConde, p. 223.
26. Dillon, p. 86.
27. Ibid.
28. De Conde, p. 233.

CHAPTER 7. AGENT 13

1. Charles Gayarri, *History of Louisiana: The Spanish Domination*, 4 vols. (New Orleans, 1879), III, 365.
2. David Leon Chandler, *The Jefferson Conspiracies: A President's Role in the Assassination of Meriwether Lewis* (New York, 1994), p. 93.
3. Roger Kennedy, *Burr, Hamilton, and Jefferson: A Study in Character* (New York, 2000), p. 114.
4. Chandler, p. 102.
5. Ibid., p. 103.
6. Ibid.
7. Ibid., p. 99.
8. Ibid., p. 85.
9. Ibid., p. 110.
10. Anonymous to Jefferson, June 26, 1801, Jefferson Papers, Library of Congress.
11. Jackson, *Jefferson*, p. 34.
12. Ibid., p. 112.
13. Ibid., p. 147.
14. Ibid., p. 244.
15. Wallace, p. 253.
16. Ibid., p. 256.
17. Ibid., p. 258.
18. Ibid., p. 259.
19. Ibid., p. 256.
20. Ibid., p. 260.
21. Ibid.
22. Chandler, p. 154.
23. Wallace, p. 262.
24. Ibid.
25. Jefferson to Priestly, January 29, 1804, Jefferson Papers, Library of Congress.
26. Jefferson to Jean Baptiste Say, February 1, 1804, Jefferson Papers, Library of Congress.
27. Wallace, p. 204.
28. Jackson, *Jefferson*, p. 245.
29. Ibid., p. 264.
30. Ibid., p. 245.

31. Jefferson to Congress, December 6, 1805, Jefferson Papers, Library of Congress.

32. Jefferson to Congress, December 3, 1805, Jefferson Papers, Library of Congress.

33. Ibid.

34. Weber, p. 292.

35. Jackson, p. 250.

36. Ibid.

37. Ibid., p. 253.

38. Ibid., p. 254.

39. Patrick Gass, *The Journals of Patrick Gass, Member of the Lewis and Clark Expedition*, edited by Carol Lynn MacGregor (Missoula, Mont., 1997), p. 151.

40. Ibid., p. 147.

41. Coues, p. 693.

42. Ibid., p. 742.

43. Bergon, p. 345.

44. Coues, p. 790.

45. Ibid., p. 720.

46. James R. Gibson, *Farming the Frontier: The Agricultural Opening of the Oregon Country, 1786–1846* (Seattle, 1985), p. 14.

47. Coues, p. 720.

48. Gass, p. 163.

49. Bergon, p. 362.

50. Coues, p. 810.

51. Ibid., p. 811.

52. Ibid., p. 818.

53. Gass, p. 168.

CHAPTER 8. THE BURR CONSPIRACY

1. Safire, p. 432.

2. Kennedy, pp. 134, 112. Thomas Fleming, *Duel: Alexander Hamilton, Aaron Burr, and the Future of America* (New York, 1999), p. 72.

3. Coues, I, 42.

4. Kennedy, p. 28.

5. Ibid., pp. 104, 257. Fleming, p. 89. Kennedy calls the resulting backlash

against black votes, from 1800 to 1820, the nation's first Jim Crow period.

6. Kennedy, p. 31.
7. Fleming, p. 142.
8. Kennedy, p. 174.
9. Ibid., p. 241. A comprehensive view of Jefferson's plans for Native Americans is laid out in Anthony F. C. Wallace, *Jefferson and the Indians.*
10. Jackson, *Jefferson,* p. 249.
11. Fleming, p. 197.
12. Kennedy, pp. 247, 100, 244.
13. Ibid., p. 251.
14. Walter Flavius McCaleb, *The Aaron Burr Conspiracy* (New York: Wilson-Erickson, 1936), p. 57.
15. Kennedy, p. 267.
16. McCaleb, p. 65.
17. Ibid., p. 57.
18. Folch to Iturrigaray, October 1, 1806, in McCaleb, p. 88.
19. McCaleb, p. 107.
20. Ibid., p. 95. Italics added.
21. Ibid., p. 96.
22. Ibid., p. 105.
23. Ibid., p. 113.
24. Ibid., p. 117.
25. DeConde, p. 236.
26. McCaleb, p. 151.
27. Ibid., p. 74.
28. Ibid., p. 75.
29. Ibid.
30. Ibid., p. 123.
31. Ibid., p. 163.
32. McCaleb, p. 153.
33. Buckner F. Melton, *Aaron Burr: Conspiracy to Treason* (New York: Wiley, 2002), p. 132.
34. McCaleb, p. 303.
35. Ibid., p. 309.
36. Ibid., p. 145.
37. Kennedy, p. 27.
38. Fleming, p. 141.

39. Kennedy, p. 134.
40. McCaleb, p. 154.
41. Jackson, *Jefferson*, p. 256.
42. Ibid., p. 257.
43. Kennedy, p. 130.
44. Jefferson to Priestly, January 29, 1804, Jefferson Papers, Library of Congress.
45. Kennedy, p. 284.

Chapter 9. Whatever Happened to Meriwether Lewis?

1. Jackson, *Letters*, p. 467.
2. Chandler, p. 44.
3. Dillon, p. 274.
4. Ibid., p. 276.
5. Ibid., p. 288.
6. Ibid., p. 297.
7. Ibid., p. 292.
8. Ibid., p. 315.
9. Ibid., p. 299.
10. Ibid., p. 315.
11. Ibid., p. 301.
12. Ibid., p. 319.
13. Ibid., p. 316.
14. Ibid., pp. 323, 306.
15. Ibid., p. 320.
16. Ibid., p. 307.
17. Ibid., p. 327.
18. Chandler, p. 278.
19. Ibid., p. 282.
20. Grace Lewis Miller letter to *William and Mary Quarterly*, December 16, 1956. Grace Lewis Miller Papers, Jefferson National Expansion Library, St. Louis, Subseries 8, Articles, Folder 14, pp. 9–10. Miller's papers are extensive and unpublished. Her unpublished thesis, "His Excellency Meriwether Lewis and the First Publications West of the Mississippi River" (University of Texas, 1948), examines Lewis's tenure as governor at St. Louis. She cites much material to support her argument that Lewis was murdered.

21. Chandler, p. 282.
22. Ibid., p. 294.
23. Ibid., pp. 296–297.
24. Dan L. Flores, ed., *Jefferson and Southwestern Exploration: The Freeman and Custis Accounts of the Red River Expedition of 1806* (Norman, Okla., 1984), pp. xvi–xvii.
25. Ibid., p. 314.
26. Jackson, *Letters*, p. 470.
27. Flores, p. 315.
28. Chandler, p. 16.
29. Paul Allen, ed., *History of the Expedition under the Command of Captains Lewis and Clark, to the Sources of the Missouri, Thence Across the Rocky Mountains and Down the River Columbia to the Pacific Ocean* (Philadelphia, 1814), pp. xxi–xxii.
30. Coues, I, xli.
31. Chandler, p. 310.
32. Coues, I, xliii.
33. Dillon, p. 337.
34. Chandler, p. 314.
35. Dillon, p. 346.
36. Chandler, p. 21.
37. Dillon, p. 336.
38. Ibid., p. 338.
39. Chandler, p. 21.
40. Dillon, p. 344.
41. Reimert Thorolf Ravenholt, "Self-Destruction on the Natchez Trace: Meriwether Lewis's Act of Ultimate Courage," *Columbia* (Summer 1999), p. 6.
42. Peter D. Sleeth, "For Now, Meriwether Lewis' Death Will Remain a Mystery," (Portland) *Oregonian*, December 17, 1997.
43. Interview on Salon.com, March 22, 1999, http://www.salon.com/it/feature/1999/03/22feature.html.
44. James E. Starrs, *Meriwether Lewis: His Death and His Monument* (privately published, 1997), p. 15. He refers to Dee Brown, "Mysteries of American History," *American Heritage*, December 1990, p. 52.
45. Telephone conversation with Richard Williams, National Park Service, Omaha, Nebr., January 11, 2002.
46. Dillon, p. xix.

CHAPTER 10. THE WREST OF THE WEST

1. Nicholas Trist to Virginia Randolph, January 16, 1822. Quoted in Wallace Ohrt, *Defiant Peacemaker: Nicholas Trist in the Mexican War* (College Station, Tex., 1997), p. 34.
2. T. C. Elliott, "Thompson, David, Introduction to the Narrative of, Relating to the Discovery of the Columbia River," *Quarterly of the Oregon Historical Society*, vol. 27, no. 1 (March 1925), 43.
3. T. C. Elliott, "The Strange Case of Thompson and Pinch," *Oregon Historical Quarterly*, vol. 40 (1939), 192.
4. Some have thought the Poltito Palton meant the Palouse nation, and the Fall Indians may have been those living near the Palouse Falls of the Palouse River, a tributary of the Snake River. Rock Lake, a large lake located in eastern Washington, has been suggested as Pinch's location. John C. Jackson locates Pinch on Flathead Lake, in western Montana, a more likely position.
5. Pinch letters found in Elliott, "Strange Case," pp. 190–191.
6. Ibid., p. 190.
7. Alvin M. Josephy, Jr., *The Nez Perce Indians and the Opening of the Northwest* (Lincoln, Nebr., 1979), p. 38.
8. Frank E. Ross, "Early Fur Trade of the Great Northwest," *Oregon Historical Quarterly*, vol. 39, no. 4 (December 1938), 398.
9. Dillon, p. 257.
10. Richard Edward Oglesby, *Manuel Lisa and the Opening of the Missouri Fur Trade* (Norman, Okla., 1963), p. 99.
11. Ohrt, pp. 28, 44.
12. Ibid., p. 53.
13. Ibid., p. 101.
14. Ibid., p. 112.
15. David M. Potter, *The Impending Crisis, 1848–1861* (New York, 1976), p. 2.
16. Ibid., p. 4.
17. Ohrt, p. 142.
18. Potter, p. 6.

Index

A NOTE ON THE AUTHOR

Laurie Winn Carlson's interests have frequently centered on the American West. Born in Sonora, California, she studied at the University of Idaho, Arizona State University, Eastern Washington University, and Washington State University. Her other books include *Cattle: An Informal Social History*; *A Fever in Salem*, a widely praised reinterpretation of the New England witch trials; *On Sidesaddles to Heaven: The Women of the Rocky Mountain Mission*; and the award-winning children's book *Boss of the Plains: The Hat That Won the West*. She is married with two sons and lives in Cheney, Washington.